— THE —
COSMIC
ALARM
CLOCK

WAKE UP TO YOUR
EXTRAORDINARY LIFE

SHARI ALDRICH

WORLDCHANGERS MEDIA

Copyright ©2024 by Shari Aldrich. All rights reserved. No part of this book may be reproduced or used in any manner without the prior written permission of the copyright owner, except for the use of brief quotations in a book review. To request permissions, contact publisher@worldchangers.media.

DISCLAIMER: This is a work of nonfiction. Nonetheless, some of the names and identifying character traits of people featured in the stories herein have been changed in order to protect their identities. Any resulting resemblance to persons either living or dead is entirely coincidental. The publisher and the Author make no representations or warranties of any kind with respect to this book or its contents, and assume no responsibility for errors, inaccuracies, omissions, or any other inconsistencies herein. The content of this book is for informational purposes only and is not intended to diagnose, treat, cure, or prevent any condition or disease, including mental health conditions. You understand that this book is not intended as a substitute for consultation with a licensed healthcare provider. The use of this book implies your acceptance of this disclaimer.

At the time of publication, the URLs displayed in this book refer to existing websites owned by Shari Aldrich and/or authors' affiliates. WorldChangers Media is not responsible for, nor should be deemed to endorse or recommend, these websites; nor is it responsible for any website content other than its own, or any content available on the internet not created by WorldChangers Media.

Paperback: 978-1-955811-77-4
E-book: 978-1-955811-78-1
LCCN: 2024910317

First paperback edition: June 2024
Editors: Audra Figgins, Paul Baillie-Lane, Samantha Ripley

Published by WorldChangers Media
PO Box 83, Foster, RI 02825
www.WorldChangers.Media

To everyone dedicated to the fight against adversity, may this book inspire you to keep waking up to your extraordinary life every single day.

PRAISE

"The 'Cosmic Alarm Clock' is a concept I love and often reference about either hitting snooze or answering it. Hint: there's much more magic when we answer it and follow our heart. Shari's story of seeming tragedy turned into triumph will help you realize how life happens 'for us' not to us."

- Yanik Silver, author of *Evolved Enterprise* and Founder of Maverick1000

"*The Cosmic Alarm Clock* is a genuine wake-up call for all of us who hit life's snooze button far too often. Shari Aldrich is a powerhouse of a human being with a story that is beyond inspirational. Rather than being crushed by a catastrophic personal setback, she used it as fuel to fire up her powerful engine, both personally and professionally. Reading this book made me feel as if I was sitting face to face with Shari, reading her eyes and feeling her emotions. The book doesn't shame the reader into feeling like they aren't doing enough. Rather it lets the reader know that 'shit happens' to everyone, and it's always up to each of us to find the next path."

- Charlie Engle, author of *Running Man*

"A transformative masterpiece that speaks directly to the heart and soul, Shari Aldrich masterfully weaves her personal journey of tragic loss and how it lead her to tremendous gain. The insights in this book will guide readers to awaken their fullest potential. This book is a call to action to embrace your inner power and step into a life of extraordinary possibilities. Shari's eloquent storytelling and how she leads you by example make this an inspiring and life-changing read. If you're ready to elevate your life, this book can serve as a guiding light."

- Kyle Emanuel Brown, Lifestyle Architect,
RapidHarmony.com

"We can sleepwalk through life or wake up to our full potential when we dare to turn trials into triumphs, failures into fortune, and adversity into advantage. Shari Aldrich's *The Cosmic Alarm Clock: Wake Up to Your Extraordinary Life* is an inspiring and empowering guide to personal transformation, with deeply personal insights and five practical pillars anyone can use right now to unlock their true potential for living a life of purpose, fulfillment, and joy. No matter the circumstances or challenges you face right now, this powerful read is what you need to turn obstacles into opportunities and live your best life."

- Melinda Wittstock, Founder and CEO, Podopolo

"In *The Cosmic Alarm Clock: Wake Up to Your Extraordinary Life*, Shari Aldrich takes the premise to my prior book *Adversitology: Overcoming Adversity When You're Hanging on by a Thread* to a whole new level. The snooze button didn't exist until 1956, and to Shari, it still doesn't! She offers a compelling and deeply personal account on how to awaken the extraordinary life that awaits. Drawing on the unique challenges Shari has faced, this book introduces five foundational pillars for living a fulfilled and resilient life. It's an inspiring guide for anyone looking to transform obstacles into opportunities and unlock their true potential."

- Frank McKinney, Real Estate Artist and 9X bestselling author of

Aspirational Thoughts • Inspirational Images

"I love this book more than I can express! It's raw, it's honest, it's deep, and above all else it's wildly inspiring. In *The Cosmic Alarm Clock*, Shari Aldrich offers a deeply personal account of her journey to becoming 'un-numb' and fully alive. This book is a must-read for anyone seeking to break free from the limitations of fear and step into a life of passion, purpose, and aliveness."

- Patrick Combs, author of *When You Are Bursting*

CONTENTS

INTRODUCTION

— The Five Pillars For Life —

October 6, 2013, was a typical fall morning in the Pacific Northwest, cold and cloudy with the promise of sun in the afternoon. For those of us who thrive in the PNW, it was the type of day we love—crisp, with blue skies and no rain.

I woke up excited to take part in a mud run with some friends. We met around seven in the morning and ate breakfast together. We spent our drive to the event listening to music and wondering about the obstacles. Mud runs are extreme outdoor races that— you guessed it—leave you completely covered in mud. You have to crawl under things and climb up others, get across balance beams, go down slides, and more, all while dealing with slimy, gritty mud. It sounds messy—and it is!—but it's also a lot of fun.

I started the obstacle course on a high—running through the mud, climbing over or under obstacles, slipping and sliding my way through the course. I was filthy and loving it. One of my shoes got sucked into the mud at one point, and I had to dig it out and put it back on, tying the knot tighter, of course.

About halfway through, I reached an obstacle that required participants to jump into water from a fifteen-foot-high platform. This type of obstacle is typical for many courses. I climbed up the wooden structure with help from my teammates. When I got to the top, there were at least fifty people standing on a six-foot-wide platform, waiting for their turn to jump into the water.

What I saw from the platform was scary enough for me to know that I didn't want to leap into the muddy water. It was chaotic. People were shouting and jumping. Others were flailing and appeared to need help.

Volunteers standing on the bank were throwing ropes into the water. I heard them calling out, "Grab the rope, grab the rope!" Yet at the top where I stood, other volunteers were still directing participants to jump off the ledge, even though there were people in the water right below. I couldn't imagine landing on someone and hurting them. What if someone fell on me while I was flailing in the water? I had a flashback to an article I'd read about someone dying under similar circumstances. I looked down at the water. It was obscured by all the mud coming off the participants, so I couldn't see into it. Fear flared in my belly.

To make matters worse, the temperature that morning was about fifty degrees. The water would be cold, and I knew that hypothermia was a very real thing. When submerged in cold water, your body temperature drops. Your heart and nervous system don't work normally. Maybe that's why so many people were struggling down in the water. I imagined that I, too, could become hypothermic if I jumped in the frigid water, my body slow to respond. All of this swirled through my head, and I expressed my concerns to a teammate. I didn't want to jump.

I asked a volunteer if there was an alternate way down, and he touched my elbow and responded, "Hurry up, you're holding up my line." Though I felt pressured to jump, I hesitated, listening to the alarm signals going off in my body.

One of my teammates leapt into the water, landing between two rescue divers who were saving someone from drowning. If she had landed on them, she could have been hurt, they could have been hurt, and perhaps the person they were trying to save could have drowned.

My fear of death felt like a very clear and present danger.

Mostly I couldn't handle the thought of my dad receiving a call telling him another one of his kids had died.

I wasn't going to jump.

I decided to retreat off the back side of the obstacle. That was going to be challenging, as the obstacle was designed to go up—not down. I held on to the side of the wooden structure and lowered myself over, but I reached a point about five feet off the ground where I couldn't continue down without letting go. I was thinking that I might hurt my ankle if I dropped down, but I couldn't continue hanging on. I let go.

That moment changed the trajectory of my life forever.

I hit the ground.

My pinky finger on my right hand hurt.

I looked down and saw a white flash of bone.

I saw red spilling over the bone and into the mud below.

I immediately covered my right hand with my other very muddy hand.

I called out, "Help! I need help!"

"What happened?" A volunteer nearby was coming over.

"I don't know—I think I ripped my finger off."

While the pain was excruciating, I didn't really think I'd ripped my finger off. I thought that maybe I'd sliced it on something that ripped the skin down to the bone. A man held my shoulders and led me toward a truck. He sat me on the truck bed and took my right hand. I rested my head on my left arm, leaned on the side of the truck, and focused on breathing. I heard snippets of conversation as the medic arrived.

"Is it ALS or BLS?"

A rush of relief washed over me when I heard the response, "Basic life support." *Advanced* was not a word you wanted to hear in a situation like this. But my mind was struggling to stay focused. I could hear my heartbeat. Different voices called back and forth, some seeming very far away.

"We have the helicopter ready if needed ..."

Focus on breathing—don't pass out.

"I found the finger."

Don't pass out—breathe in, breathe out.

"I dropped the finger in the mud."

That information felt important to remember. *Just keep breathing—don't pass out.* Someone was wrapping something around my hand.

"You're doing great ..."

"Let's get her to the medic tent."

We drove to the medic tent in a golf cart. People's faces were blurry. I saw a couple of participants with warming blankets on their shoulders. I thought that possibly they were hypothermic—or injured. I didn't ask. I focused on my breathing.

An ambulance arrived. I was helped onto a stretcher and rolled into the back. It was slow-going, the vehicle slamming into the ruts of the muddy dirt road over and over and over until we got to pavement. I felt far away, but I talked with the paramedic about my pain, which I quantified with an 8 on a 1–10 scale.

In the emergency room, I was taken for X-rays and given hydromorphone for the pain. I felt an immediate *whoosh* through my body as the drug shot into my veins like a rush of adrenaline, that fight-or-flight feeling when you know something bad is about to happen.

I felt that I was a conscious observer through the whole process. One part of my brain was processing what was happening to me; the other part was observing the medical treatment and fascinated by the process.

I saw the back of a nurse for most of my time in the room. In the beginning, I wasn't sure what she was doing. She was standing at a counter, working on something.

After some time, the doctor arrived. He was a hand specialist, and the hospital had called him in on a Sunday to look at my hand and make recommendations. He told me that I had "degloved" my finger, meaning that, while the bones were still attached, the skin, tendons, blood vessels, muscles, and nerves had been ripped off. He held his hands about eight or nine inches apart to show how much tissue had been removed.

He then told me that the nurse with her back to me had been cleaning the rest of the finger. My finger. The one that was not attached to my hand. Oh right, I remembered—someone had mentioned my finger being dropped in the mud back at the obstacle course.

Looking at the X-rays, the doctor shared that my finger bone had also been broken in three places. He advised me that he could try to reattach everything if I wanted, but that if he did, he would have to create a pocket in my belly to hold my finger for a couple of weeks to see if the skin would regenerate.

The finger had been dropped in the mud. What if the nurse missed a microscopic bacterium that was then introduced into my body? And even if that part went well, what then were the risks to my life if I decided to do the surgery and have everything reattached?

These thoughts swirled sluggishly. I was lying in the hospital bed and couldn't feel my right hand at all. The nurse continued her task. The doctor gave me a 0 percent chance that reattaching my finger would work.

Then, this doctor—a hand-specialist surgeon who relied on the dexterous capabilities of his hands and fingers to help people every day—said to me, "Given there's zero chance of reattaching your finger, if I were in your position, I would tell the doctor to remove it."

Fear of death has been a major focus of my thoughts for many years.

Maybe it was growing up during the Cold War, when the threat of nuclear bombings was made real through air-raid drills held in school, sirens blaring as warning systems were tested, after-school movies about nuclear war, and commercials on TV. Then there was anxiety about Y2K. A lot of folks thought the world was going to end, and I remember lying awake at night as a kid thinking that in the year 2000 I would be only thirty-four years old, watching the world burn or drown or explode.

When I was eleven, I saw my mom soak an entire hand towel with her tears when her mom died at just fifty-six years old. I was in my early twenties when my dad's parents died. From my early perspective, life was very short. For as long as I can remember, I've been afraid of dying at a young age. What if my mom soaked a hand towel for me? I held a lot of anxiety around dying early, and I now realize it's because I didn't want to cause my mom to suffer if something happened to me.

I made it to my thirties, and while the world continued on, my personal world suffered serious losses. Half of my core family died.

My brother, Steve, was thirty-six years old when he died of a stroke in 1997.

My mom, Sharon, was fifty-nine years old when she died from lung cancer in 2000. We found out her diagnosis on a Saturday, and she died the following Monday. The doctor said it was a wildfire in her lungs.

My older sister, Judi, was thirty-nine years old when she died in a car accident in 2004, leaving behind her two young children.

These were all unexpected deaths that left me with zero time to adjust or adapt. The most important people in my life were vanishing, and my dad, Jack, my younger sister, Janice, and I were left picking up the pieces. But it felt more like trying to hold water in your hand; everything just kept slipping away.

After my older sister's death, I would wake up in a cold sweat thinking how sad it would be for me to die before I was forty, leaving my two kids—Hayley, fifteen, and Ashleigh, thirteen—to grow up without a mom. The fear was very real. I loved my job for the challenges it offered, but at the same time, it felt meaningless. I had daily headaches and stress. I was taking ten to twelve ibuprofen every day just to get by.

I was living to die, not living to live. And what kind of life is that?

After my accident on that mud run course, I finally stopped running from fear. Since that day, I have learned how to turn the tables on fear and use it as a catalyst for living with joy. Fear is not something I will ever fully get rid of, but it no longer stops me from experiencing and enjoying my life. It has even helped me navigate some of life's most difficult moments.

During the COVID-19 pandemic, I created my Five Pillars for Life concept, which helps guide me when making decisions. It makes it easy when I'm faced with a problem to solve. It includes:

Become Un-Numb: Sometimes needing to make a decision is like a wake-up call. Becoming un-numb is about mindfully noticing when you've become complacent. So when faced with a decision, I ask myself, *Am I drifting through life, accepting what comes my way? By making this decision, will I be taking decisive action to create a better opportunity for myself?*

Movement Is Life: This has become my life mantra. When you think about it, everything about life is movement! You don't get anywhere by standing still, and stagnancy doesn't offer new opportunities. So I ask myself next, *Does this create movement for me or my business?*

Follow Your Joy: After losing most of my family, I learned that the only way to get up out of bed and sustain movement is to follow the joy path—if I do something, it needs to bring me joy. Asking, *Does this decision help me follow my joy?* is a great way to feel out if a choice is the right one.

Move the Boat: Fear is the ultimate antimotivator. When I've been afraid in the past, I've let that fear stop me from moving forward. But when you're sitting in a boat, if you don't stick your oar in the water and row, the water is going to push you wherever it wants to go. So I ask myself, *By making this decision, am I the one moving the boat? Or am I letting myself be pushed by the waves?*

Tell Your Story: Finally, my archetype is a storyteller, so I love to use story to connect to people. I have found that story brings people together by building empathy and community. When we understand one another better, we can work together toward a better life for all of us. So I ask myself, *Does making this decision align with the story I want to tell?*

What follows in these pages is my personal story, and each part of it is represented by one of these pillars, the foundations upon which I now base all my decisions. One thing I have learned over the years of dealing with trauma and pain is that healing is a journey. There is no one-size-fits-all solution, no magic pill that will take away all your pain. Healing is a practice of moving forward, one step at a time.

While it's true that everyone's healing journey is unique, one thing that is common to all of us is the experience of loss. Whether it's loss of a loved one, a relationship, a job, or one's health, the pain and grief that accompany loss can be a profound and universal human experience.

I've often wondered why loss can be so painful and whether it's possible to find meaning and growth in the midst of our suffering. While there are no easy answers, I believe that by staying open to the lessons and opportunities that arise from our losses, we can begin to heal and grow in ways that we never thought possible. We tend to fall into patterns when we're in pain. But, as they say, the definition of insanity is trying the same thing over and over and expecting a different result.

The purpose of this book, of sharing my story, is to help you through your own personal healing journey. Today I'm a strong, resilient leader and courageous risk-taker—but I wasn't always like that. I was hampered by grief and fear and pain for many years, stuck in what I thought I was supposed to do and who I thought I was supposed to be. But that is no way to live.

If you are suffering and in pain today, my hope is that, as you read, my story will help you find your inner strength and develop your own pillars to make clear decisions and thrive through difficult times. Now is the time to find your own path toward healing, climb that ladder toward your version of success, and discover the life you are meant to live. Once you've climbed some distance, you can then turn around and hold out your hand, helping and inspiring others to find their healing path too.

So take my hand, and let's start building a plan to keep moving forward together, one step at a time.

PILLAR #1

— Become Un-Numb —

ONE

When my mom was pregnant with me, she told my brother, Steve, that I would be a boy, since he already had a sister. Obviously I wasn't a boy, but my brother treated me as if I were my whole life. He taught me to play baseball, basketball, and football. I was often outside playing sports with him and the neighborhood kids until I started playing school sports.

I played three sports in high school—soccer, basketball, and softball. I was also a very good athlete. Years of playing competitive sports helped me develop traits that I still value, such as a team-player attitude, discipline, perseverance, leadership, resiliency, and respect.

I remember one basketball game we played against a rival team on their home court. My team was down by two points with three seconds left in the game. We had to take the ball from the far end of the court against heavy defense and make the basket to tie the game.

We missed the shot. Game over.

Dejected, we went to the locker room and started getting ready for the long bus ride home. Suddenly, our coach came into the locker room and told us we were going to get to replay the last seconds of the game again, because it turned out that their clock had burnt-out bulbs—there were really eight seconds left in the game, not three!

When we returned to the court, most of the fans had left already. However, I looked in the stands and saw my mom and my aunt still there. My mom was my biggest cheerleader, supporting me at every game.

We once again took the ball from the far end of the court and now, emboldened by the second chance, made the basket and tied the game.

The game went to triple overtime, and we won! The team went wild; we were jumping up and down and hugging each other. My mom and aunt, who were two of the few fans left to see this miracle happen, cheered right along with us.

The bus ride home was jubilant. When we got back to the high school, many parents who had left the game thinking we had lost were wondering why it took the bus so long to get home. This experience cemented early for me the truth of the saying—perhaps best said by the baseball player Yogi Berra—"It ain't over till it's over."

While my mom always encouraged and supported me in whatever I wanted to do, it was my dad, Jack, who role modeled taking chances and living life to the fullest. He grew up in Iowa, where his grandpa owned a dairy farm. Jack's dad was expected to work that farm first before going home to work his own dairy farm at the end of the day. It must have been an exhausting life. When Jack was thirteen, his dad had an opportunity to buy a dairy farm in Centralia, Washington. He packed up and took the family across the country to start a new life.

I would wager that Jack recognized how big of a risk his dad took by embarking on a cross-country move in the 1950s, buying property far away from any support system, and building a dairy farm from the ground up. My dad grew up farming, but when he graduated high school he, like his father before him, wanted to get as far away as possible. After working at a drugstore as a teenager, he decided to go to college to become a pharmacist.

Jack was later drafted in the Vietnam War, which derailed his life plans for a while. But when he came home, he reenrolled in college and worked three jobs to put himself through school—with a wife and four kids at home. He graduated and began a long career as a pharmacist in many cities in Idaho and Washington State. What a role model he was!

My parents, high school sweethearts, were married for forty-one years. They tied the knot on my mom's nineteenth birthday, just months after she graduated high school. Back then, their school dances had dance cards where you'd record the name of the people you intended to dance with for each song. I came across one of my mom's dance cards, and every dance had *Jack* on the line. They were always meant to be together.

My dad always dreamed of owning a drug store in a ski resort, and after all of us kids graduated from high school, he acted on that dream and bought a store in Crested Butte, Colorado. Every day during ski season, he closed the store and skied for two hours. From him, I saw firsthand how following your bliss can make you so incredibly happy, but it wasn't until later in my life that I would fully learn that lesson and embrace it as my dad had.

We had a family joke growing up. My mom hated the snow and my dad hated the rain. Living in western Washington, we saw a lot of rain. We imagined our dad waking up every morning saying, "Shit, rain again." After my parents moved to Colorado, we imagined our mom waking up every morning saying, "Shit, snow again."

Honestly, though, they did okay in Colorado. My mom hated being away from her family but knew that my dad was happy there. They made it about four years before my dad sold the business and they moved back to Washington in 1989. The seasonality of the business was not sustainable—busy in the winter and extremely slow in the summer.

I truly do not think I was ever asked to consider what I wanted to do when I graduated from high school. So I tried college, but after eighteen months, I dropped out. It wasn't for me. I didn't have a clear idea of what I wanted to do with my life. I moved to Colorado to live with my parents for about six months during this time.

I thought I had to follow the same path as everyone else: graduate from school, get a job, get married, and have babies. Though I hadn't completed the school part, at nineteen I went home to Washington, got a job at a photofinishing lab, met my husband, Arlin, and started a family. I had my first baby, a girl we named Hayley, in 1989 and a second daughter, Ashleigh, in 1991. My mom loved being a grandma. When I told her I was pregnant, she cried for about a minute before getting busy with the grandma things about two minutes later, like buying baby clothes and diapers.

Arlin and I bought a house across the street from my parents, and for several years my kids spent every day after school with my mom. She taught my girls how to sew. She had dinner made for us when I got home from work. It was amazing, and I felt so grateful to be so close to her and able to share my life with her.

Losing my mom in 2000 was devastating for everyone. She was the anchor of our family. She organized everything—from holiday parties to family reunions. She made fancy birthday cakes for her grandkids. She had the most well-decorated Christmas tree every year with lots of sparkling lights, mirrors, and gold balls.

In the spring of 2000, she went to the doctor because she had been having abdominal pain for a while. They took X-rays of her abdomen and did blood work. At first the doctor told her that it was her appendix causing the pain, and though they scheduled her for surgery, the appendix was ruled out as the problem before it took place. Then they noticed that she had fluid in her belly, took a sample, and tested it for abnormalities, including cancer. The fluid came back negative.

The doctors took another X-ray, this time focusing more on her lungs. Testing still came back negative for cancer, and they began testing for tuberculosis. My mom was transferred to a larger hospital, and while waiting for results from the TB test, everyone was required to wear a face mask around her. She started on breathing treatments, as it was becoming evident that the problem was in her lungs, not her abdomen.

Eventually, TB was ruled out. It was decided that she would have surgery to remove a wedge section of her lungs so they could test that tissue to diagnose what was wrong. A surgeon told us to tell her goodbye, because her condition was worsening and he didn't know if she would survive the surgery.

As we were surrounding our mom and telling her we loved her, the surgeon came back and said that a lab test revealed a cell the size of a pin had come back positive for small cell lung cancer, and it was very aggressive. The doctor had shown me three X-rays: In April, an X-ray that primarily focused on her abdomen showed the bottom of her lungs, and they were clear. On May 27, the X-ray focusing on her chest had a light sprinkling of white dots at the lower part of her lungs. On June 3—just one week later—the X-ray showed massive white splotches throughout both lungs.

We were all devastated. My dad was stoic in front of us girls and didn't show much emotion, but I know he was broken by this news. Janice, Judi, and I did our best to stay positive for our mom.

The doctor said that a round of chemotherapy might give her a few more weeks to live, but there wasn't going to be a cure. She chose to have chemotherapy and started it that day. Janice and I stayed with her in the hospital overnight while she was receiving chemo via IV. In the middle of the night she had to use the bathroom, and Janice and I did our best to help her without calling for the nurse. We managed to get her standing up and were just hugging and loving her—a lovely moment—when she said she really had to pee. We all laughed. It's a precious memory for me to this day.

In the end, she didn't get any extra weeks to live. She never even left the hospital. She died two days later, surrounded by me, my sisters, our dad, and my husband. Being there for her was something I will never forget. One nurse told us that every death is different: some people want to die alone or just with their spouse; some people want to be surrounded by their large, extended family; and some people want to die with their immediate family. Throughout the day, we offered my mom these scenarios, as we knew the end was near. A nurse took Janice and me aside and told us not to be afraid in the moment of her death—that it would be "the closest heaven and earth come together." In the end, my mom passed quietly in the middle of the night with her immediate family by her side, all of us telling her we loved her.

After our mom died, we sisters did our best to be there for our dad. We were pretty proud of ourselves on the first Christmas without her, taking on the "Mom always bought these" gifts—socks, T-shirts, and underwear for our dad. We made the holiday dinner and spent as much time with him as we could that first year.

But life doesn't stop. Time moved on, and after she was gone, my dad was searching for his footing in the world. My parents had loved to travel. They especially enjoyed skiing and gambling. A common vacation for them was one week in Mexico for the sun and warmth followed by a week in Lake Tahoe where my dad would ski and my mom would gamble. Some time after her death, he felt the itch to get back out in the world and reached out to friends from Colorado, soon joining several adventure groups as a medic. He found himself fishing in South America and Alaska and went on a rafting trip in Colorado in a group that included Jimmy Carter and his Secret Service crew. That experience led to a trip with the same crew (sans Jimmy Carter), and they flew on a floatplane from Alaska to Siberia—where they had to land in the ocean to refuel.

My dad taught me grit, resiliency, and to follow my dreams.

In 2005, my dad took my daughter Hayley to Europe for five weeks. One day while in Saint Petersburg, Russia, my dad was sitting on the hotel patio drinking a beer and reading a book while Hayley was upstairs in the hotel room watching TV. A woman approached my dad and asked if she could join him; she also wanted to drink a beer and read a book, and since every other table was full, she asked to sit at his.

They had a lovely chat that sunny afternoon, my dad learning that the woman was named Hilly and that she was from the Netherlands. It was her first trip traveling alone since her divorce. At one point, Hayley thought my dad had been gone a long time, so she went downstairs to check on him. He and Hilly were chatting like they were old friends already.

The next morning, my dad and Hilly found each other again and exchanged contact information. With that, they began a long-distance relationship for a couple of years. At least once or twice a year they would travel to visit each other.

In 2007, just before Thanksgiving, Hilly was visiting the US. Coming through customs, she was questioned at length about why she was traveling here so often, and she thought they were going to stick her on a plane and send her back to the Netherlands.

This resulted in my dad and Hilly deciding to get married over that Thanksgiving weekend. As we speedily made plans for a wedding, Hilly's daughter, Kim, reached out to me over email for the first time and planned a surprise: she was going to fly to the States along with Hilly's sister, Karen, and son, Arjan, for the wedding on Thanksgiving weekend. It was difficult to keep this secret from my dad and Hilly, but I loved meeting my new stepfamily.

When Hilly knocked on the door for Thanksgiving dinner, Kim answered, and Arjan recorded his mom's reaction. She was stunned silent for a few seconds trying to figure out this strange sight! But joy and hugs ensued, and we had an amazing Thanksgiving meal.

Sharing our family traditions with Hilly's family was special, as they had never tasted some of the food before—such as sweet potatoes!

The wedding was held on the Saturday after Thanksgiving. It was a small affair with immediate family and a few family friends. It was certainly a celebration, but there were also moments where we sisters remembered our mom and the life we'd had with her.

When my dad and Hilly reported their wedding to the government, they were penalized for not applying for a fiancée visa prior to getting married. Hilly had to leave the country for a year until everything was resolved—a costly error on many fronts, including lawyers and the emotions of separation.

My dad returned to the Netherlands for a second wedding there at Hilly's church. Her family and friends and my sister Janice and I attended. The wedding there was quite a bit different! The service was held in both Dutch and English so we could understand. Once the service was over, the chairs were removed and bistro-style tables were situated around the church for food and beer. When the church closed for the day, we continued the party at my stepsister's house until the wee hours of the morning.

What I loved most about this time was that my dad was happy again. He fully embodied the idea of living in joy despite what he'd been through, and this was always a huge inspiration for me. It also made clear to me the fact that families can be made in many ways. Arjan became like a true brother to me, and had my dad not taken the risk on a new relationship, I would have missed knowing him and gaining a brother after so much loss.

My dad passed away in 2018. Losing him was devastating, like losing my anchor. He died doing what he loved: he was puttering in his garage with a cold beer in his hands when he had a massive heart attack and was gone.

In my life, I can say that my dad was a role model for following his joy. He loved Hilly until he passed away. He skied until the doctors told him he shouldn't anymore due to Ménière's disease, which causes vertigo. He traveled extensively his whole life. He loved his little farm and took care of fruit trees, chickens, and sometimes cows. He came back from multiple surgeries and remained active until the day he died. He refused to live in numbness, and that inspired me to do the same.

TWO

I got a job in 1985 as a receptionist with a small home health and hospice agency. Over the years, I progressed through the company, moving from reception to medical records to hospice team coordinator.

One day we were sitting in a meeting with the leadership team. The president of the company had decided to separate us from a franchise, creating an employee-owned company. New positions would be created, and some previous ones would be eliminated. He was going around the table and assigning jobs—pointing to someone who would be the director, someone who would be the records manager, and so on.

Then he asked, "Who's going to do the computers?" I looked around the room, and no one raised their hand. I felt a fire burst to life inside of me and raised my hand, even though I really had no idea how to "do the computers." This was a pivotal moment, one of the first times that I did the unexpected and took a chance, pushing past fear and self-limitations toward real personal growth.

I became the IT person in the new company in 1999. I had zero experience or skills, but I dug right in, trying to understand how network printers worked. In my mind, I just pictured a mess of twenty cables going from each computer to the printer. I didn't understand how switches or hubs worked. This was in the early days of home computers when they were large and bulky. The internet was not widely used yet. My husband, Arlin, worked with computers every day, and we did have one at home, but it was mostly used for email, simple word processing, and games for our kids to play. A larger network in a business was foreign to me.

It was clear I was mostly on my own, and the majority of my IT education was achieved by pure determination on my part. I worked with the software company behind our medical records program to get an understanding of the processes involved in creating and using electronic medical records. My husband worked in an environment that was on the cutting edge of technology, so I consulted with him to get ideas about best practices with hardware. It was challenging to learn this new technology, but I found that I was really enjoying myself.

I was the IT director for seven years, and it was truly the best of times and the worst of times. I loved learning new technology, especially as it became clear that computers were the future. I enjoyed the status I gained by the title—and the pay.

On the downside, I was on call 24-7, and there was always something going wrong. I was being pulled in so many different directions by staff who needed technical support, people who didn't grow up using technology the way we do today. But I was only one person, and I couldn't be everywhere I was needed. Once I was bowling in the Women's National Bowling Tournament in Reno, Nevada, and I had to leave and stand outside on the phone to troubleshoot computer problems for a new staff person. Other times, I had to troubleshoot connectivity problems for people who lived in remote areas without internet service.

In addition, while working in hospice was special, it became much more difficult for me after my brother and mom died. Hearing about death and dying every day was hard. I developed a fear-based hypochondria, thinking that every bump and bruise I had was cancer. But I was so terrified at the thought of the diagnosis that I never had any tests done. I fretted about my own death every day.

During this time, I had massive stress and developed excruciating daily headaches. I took upward of twelve ibuprofen every day. I was eating junk food, as there was never time to cook proper meals. I gained weight due to anxiety and poor diet. I had insomnia, and this was when the dreams started—the ones about dying before I was forty, leaving my kids to grow up without a mom. I cried for them. I would struggle to fall asleep at night. Or I would fall asleep only to wake up again an hour later and lay there awake.

I was doing my best, yet feeling like it wasn't enough.

I knew this was no way to live, but I didn't see a way out. Sure, my job was stressful, but I was earning a better-than-average income for the community I lived in. There were two kids at home whose futures I constantly had in the back of my mind. I thought I was living the way I was supposed to: get married, have kids, and go to a real, corporate, nine-to-five job each day to support the family. But while I was outwardly successful, there was no heart in what I did. I had worked hard to get to that point, but I would find myself wondering, *What is it all for*? I was rudderless and stressed.

By the end of 2003, I was ready for a change.

THREE

The first time my cosmic alarm clock rang was at 5:00 a.m. on a cold morning in January of 2004. By *cosmic alarm clock*, I don't mean an actual alarm clock decorated with planets and stars. I mean the insistent inner feeling that pushes you in a certain direction that can seem so out of the blue that it must be coming from some higher cosmic power.

I woke up that morning with a vision that I needed to run a marathon. I had no idea where that came from, as I'd never been a distance runner—ever. In fact, I'd wanted to continue playing soccer into college, but my brother told me that the team ran five miles a day, and it scared me off. I didn't think I could run that distance. I let that belief stop me from playing a sport I truly loved.

This message from the universe was so strong that I had to listen to it despite my misgivings. Imagine waking up from a dead sleep with a message to start training for a marathon and a voice saying, *Don't even think about it. Get up. Get dressed. Go run.*

The voice was compelling. I didn't know why, but I felt like I should listen to it. So I got dressed, went outside, and jog-walked a half-mile. The next day, I went one mile.

Every morning, my mantra was *Don't even think about it. Get up. Get dressed. Go run.*

After a few weeks, five miles became my normal daily run. I changed my diet. I stopped eating sugar. I stopped eating a lot of wheat. I began to feel like me again.

Deepening my commitment to run a marathon, I signed up for the 2004 Seattle Marathon, which is held the Sunday after Thanksgiving every year. I chose the Seattle Marathon because the date was far enough out from when I first decided to run that I would have enough time to train. I began reading articles about marathon training, but mostly I just ran every morning.

Two months into my training, I walked into a health food store and learned that a massage therapist was renting a room there, and that day, he was offering free sports massages to build his clientele. I didn't know what to expect, as I'd never had a sports massage, but I signed up. He stretched out my glutes and did compression on my legs and back. It felt so good. After two months of running between twenty and thirty miles every week, having someone stretch my sore muscles felt therapeutic and needed.

When he asked if I wanted a full-body massage the next week at his main office, I immediately said yes.

I really thought it would be another hour of stretching. I arrived for my appointment and filled out the intake form. He explained that I would go into the treatment room, take off my clothes down to my comfort level, and get between the sheets on the massage table.

"I don't think I'm comfortable with that!" I said, a petrified expression filling my face. Growing up, I was averse to touch—no hugs, thank you very much. He laughed, probably because I looked so terrified. He was warm and easygoing though, and I remembered how much better I'd felt after the stretching. I could do this. I wasn't going to let my fear take away this opportunity.

In the soothing, dimly-lit room, I took my clothes off and climbed face down between the sheets. He came in and put a bolster under my ankles. He compressed my back and then pulled back the blanket and sheets. When he put his hands on my back and started working, I had an epiphany: massage was what I'd been looking for my whole life! I immediately made massages a weekly necessity.

From all the running, massages, stretching, and healthy eating, I was feeling so much better. I could finally sleep and stopped having headaches altogether. I didn't need the ibuprofen at all anymore. These physical improvements led to mental ones, and I found I could handle the stress at work much better too.

For the first time in a long time, I started wondering if there could be more to life for me beyond just my corporate career. Could I do something I was really passionate about? It seemed too big and scary to think about, so I kept focusing on my smaller goal of completing my first marathon.

FOUR

On March 24, 2004, my older sister, Judi, was driving on the freeway when she was involved in a head-on collision. She and the woman driving the other car both died instantly.

As kids, Judi and I used to have massive fights. Who knows now what we fought over—we were very different from each other. She loved loud music and was eccentric. I was sporty. We clashed, but then we grew up—literally and figuratively—and became much closer. We both got married and had kids. She was a stay-at-home mom for many of her kids' early years, and I was lucky that she also loved to babysit my kids when they were young. She was a great mom who did amazing arts and crafts activities with her kids that would be the envy of Pinterest today. Her kids were nine and fifteen when she died.

Judi once said, "I don't want to be vanilla pudding; I want to be raspberry yogurt." That described her so well. She could be wild, loud, and funny. She embellished stories. She had a large, lush garden in her backyard with fruits, vegetables, and flowers. She was a good cook. She created our family Christmas tea party and cookie exchange, a tradition we all still treasure. She was a homebody who could party with the best of them.

When she was ready to start a career, she became a pharmacy tech, learning the ropes from our dad. She had divorced her husband and gone from stay-at-home mom to working mom of two kids. On the day she died, she was driving to work. We'll never know exactly what happened, but somehow, she crossed over the median and hit a car going the other direction.

Janice and I were in a lot of pain, but it nearly caused our dad to shut down. He had already lost his first child and his wife.

Dad was in no shape to make decisions, so I took over. My husband and I offered to raise her kids, even meeting with a lawyer to check into the feasibility of gaining custody, but their dad wanted to raise them. Instead, my lawyer suggested I become the executor of her estate, which required that I manage her life insurance policy as well as the house, which became the property of the kids. Their dad had physical custody, but I had financial responsibility until they reached eighteen years old. With all the spinning plates and too much grief overwhelming my body and mind, I stopped running.

Once the funeral was over and the estate dealt with, though, I began feeling like running the marathon was an imperative. I felt it would save my life. But now, it was like starting over. Getting back into the groove of running was difficult—more difficult than it had been to start at the beginning of the year.

My mantra served me well again: *Don't even think about it. Get up. Get dressed. Go run.*

I also got back into my weekly massages, which greatly helped my emotional well-being. I was able to let go of the need to solve the problems of my niece and nephew. Training for the marathon became cathartic, and running allowed me to process grief in a way that made sense to me—it kept me moving. From the lens of being afraid of dying, running made me feel alive! My massage therapist talked to me about the profession and said I'd make an excellent massage therapist.

"Why do you think that?" I asked.

"Well, because you're an athlete," he said, "you understand how the body moves."

I had to admit that was true.

He added that because I had endured a lot of sports injuries, I understood how to rehab. Also true. I had completely ruptured my anterior cruciate ligament (ACL) in my knee and had two surgeries as a result. I had torn three ligaments in my ankle in high school. I had countless sprained ankles playing basketball. Rehabbing injuries was something I was very familiar with. I was intrigued, but it didn't seem like something I could really build a career out of. I had a family to think about, and the cons seemed to outweigh the pros.

One day, my massage therapist told me how much money could be made in his profession, and that is when I really started listening.

This service, something that had helped bring me back to life, had the potential to allow me to shake off the golden handcuffs of my IT job. Suddenly, there were a lot more checks in the pros column.

The thought of making my own schedule was appealing. Not being on call 24-7 sounded even better. Earning as much (if not more) money than I was earning in IT sounded perfect. It was feeling more and more like a true answer to a dream I hadn't even known I'd dared to dream—a dream that was steadily replacing the nightmare I had every night where I died before I was forty.

I had a lot of trepidation, but I didn't want to regret not trying it out. I thought of my dad, skiing during his long lunch breaks with the biggest smile on his face. I asked the fear that was ready to pounce and crush my dreams, *What's the harm in just giving it a try? I don't have to make any changes right away.* So I went to an introductory workshop at a local massage school and fell in love with massage therapy that day. I was all in; I wanted to begin school and become a massage therapist. The next class was scheduled to start three months after the Seattle Marathon in November, which felt like perfect timing. Now I understood that the cosmic alarm clock going off that morning in January had had a bigger plan for me in mind all along. I finally felt like I was running toward something.

It was cathartic to go for a long run on the weekends. I felt that this marathon was a mission that I needed to complete by myself, for myself. And too soon, race day arrived.

At the starting line, a woman looked at me and asked, "Are you excited?" For some reason, I started bawling. I felt so emotional in that moment, thinking of my older siblings and how neither of them had made it to forty. I thought of my mom and seeing her face light up as she cheered me on at different sporting events across the years. It felt immense to be here, in this moment, just as I was, with the three of them gone. Tears streamed down my face. The woman looked at me strangely and turned away to talk to someone else.

While I was proud of how far I'd come, I thought my training hadn't been the best. I hadn't joined a running club or found a coach. Then, after my sister died, it took a while to get back on track. At first, I beat myself up about it, constantly comparing my performance to where I'd been before. But eventually I surrendered to just doing what I could every day. Some days, every step was a struggle, but I kept going. Still, a marathon is 26.2 miles, and the farthest I had run prior to that day was thirteen miles.

Don't even think about it. Get up. Get dressed. Go run.

Attempting to double my miles in one day probably wasn't the best decision. At one point, around mile seventeen, I was walking and feeling sorry for myself when an older man went running past me with a very pronounced limp, and I thought, *He is* not *going to beat me.* So I started running again.

I turned a corner at mile twenty and saw the biggest hill on the course. I started crying. I mean, who puts a massive hill in a marathon at mile twenty? I sucked it up and pushed on to the theme from *Rocky*, which was playing loudly on a speaker that someone had installed at the top of the hill.

The last two miles were a gradual decline, and all I remember thinking was: *I can definitely do twenty more minutes of running to save my life.*

Just in front of the finish line, a woman called out to me, "Look up and smile when you finish; they're going to take your picture!" I started crying again, wishing my mom, brother, and sister were there with me. But I got a great boost when I saw my kids and Arlin waiting at the finish with big smiles on their faces. Hayley ran onto the course and across the finish line with me. I *did* smile when I ran across the finish line!

Crossing the finish line of my first marathon was an exhilarating mix of astonishment and exhaustion. I felt a sense of personal triumph. Every muscle fiber was sore, but the sensation felt like a testament to the effort I'd put in over the last eleven months. The pride I felt at my accomplishment filled me with joy. It was more than fatigue that washed over me; it was the realization that I had pushed myself beyond what I thought were my limits. I was full of endorphins and emotion. I felt relief in achieving something truly momentous. In the days after completing the marathon, I understood that I had not just completed a physical journey but had learned more about myself and my ability to do difficult things.

FIVE

Four months later, in March of 2005, I started massage school at Bodymechanics School of Myotherapy and Massage and began my next chapter with excitement and curiosity. Actually, it felt like more than a new chapter, like I was cracking the spine of a brand-new book. I knew that massage therapy had been a huge reason why I'd come to life over the last year despite the trauma of another major family loss. I was eager to learn the techniques and skills that would enable me to help others the way I'd been helped.

There are two things I knew on the first day of school: I never wanted another boss ever again, and to make this work I had to earn as much money as I did in IT. Those two rules laid the foundation for my future.

Massage school was a transformative experience. The coursework was intense and demanding, requiring both physical and mental stamina, but I was determined to master the material and become the best massage therapist I could be. As I progressed through the program, I gained confidence in my skills and developed a deep appreciation for the power of touch and its ability to heal and soothe.

There's an intensity that's specific to learning body arts like massage—it's incredibly intimate and brings out everyone's individual vulnerabilities. It's one thing to attend a class with someone; it's something completely different when you remove your clothing for them to massage you. This is where the vulnerabilities really come out—especially around how you feel about your body. But before you think it's weird, it's not. People who go to massage school tend to lead with a desire to help others feel better, and that was certainly true of my fellow classmates and me. We all saw working with one another as opportunities to learn and grow, and even developed a great support system along the way.

Before I started massage school, I imagined class as just practicing massage. It turns out there's a lot of science behind massage! We studied subjects such as anatomy, physiology, and pathology to understand the body and its functions in greater depth. We learned about the muscles, where they connected on the bones and what their actions were. Knowing how the body was supposed to work gave us a greater understanding of what dysfunction looked like, so we could focus on those areas for our clients. There were practical safety matters, such as working with and around any preexisting conditions a client might have. It was also a study in understanding

31

people—a bit like a traditional therapist! We learned how to interview clients and get their health history to help us formulate their care plan.

We also learned how to run a massage practice, and I found that I loved learning about business. One of the projects was putting together a plan for a fictitious business, and I surprised myself by having quite an aptitude for this aspect of the course. I named my fictitious business Marathon Massage as a nod to my life-changing marathon the previous fall.

Many of my classmates were like me: working a day job, caring for their families, and going to night school to transform themselves by learning about massage. Trying to fit in study time around other obligations became a challenge for me, and I felt guilty when family time was the thing that got dropped. Both of my girls played softball, and I spent many weekends at the softball fields during their tournaments. I would take my massage table and practice on the kids between games, which meant I got some practice in *and* some quality time with my girls. I didn't know it at the time, but I was utilizing a technique that the motivational speaker Tony Robbins calls N.E.T. time—No Extra Time—where you stack activities to accomplish more in the day. I've used this concept a lot in my life, such as running while listening to books or podcasts.

One of the last things we did for massage school was an externship. I created a hospice caregiver massage program. Having spent time around caregivers in the hospice industry, I knew how fatiguing that necessary work could be. Being able to offer physical relief felt like a beautiful way to honor those who help the dying. I worked on nurses, social workers, nurses' aides, and sometimes the dying patients' families. This was also a way to view death and dying as a natural part of life, more positively and less fearfully than the way I had viewed death growing up and experienced death in my own family. Hospice gives the person who is dying and their family time to say goodbye, which was not my experience at all with the sudden, traumatic deaths in my family.

Prior to attending Bodymechanics, I didn't know I was an entrepreneur. I had never thought about owning my own business. I thought that after graduating I would work at my day job and build my business in the evenings and on the weekends. But fate had something different in mind for me when Janice was diagnosed with stage 3 breast cancer. I was immediately scared for her and for our family. We'd already been through so much.

Growing up, Janice was my best friend, my twin. We aren't actually twins, but we're eleven months apart—for nineteen days of the year, we are the same age. During those nineteen days as kids, we would wake up saying, "Good morning, Twin!" We still do this today.

As kids, we shared a bedroom, and even though we had separate beds, we slept in the same bed most nights. I was always the one asking if I could sleep in bed with her. We often played "I spy" before falling asleep.

When I was three, I fell and cracked my chin open, and my dad took me to the ER for stitches. He told me that if I was good and didn't cry, he would get me an ice cream cone on the way home. A few hours later, I walked into the house with an ice cream cone— no tears from me! Janice took one look at me and the ice cream and started crying. She said that she was so worried and thought I had died, and then here I came, strolling in just fine with ice cream to boot. Seeing her tears, I had to share my hard-earned ice cream with her. To hear both of our sides of the story makes me laugh.

Janice and I have always looked out for each other and worried about each other for as long as I can remember. When she was in treatment for her cancer getting a lumpectomy and radiation, she asked me about pain she was having in her neck and upper back. She was seeing a massage therapist, and I recommended she talk with him about some massage treatment ideas.

At the time of her diagnosis, Janice was working as director of housing for Western Colorado University in Gunnison, Colorado. She had her PhD in Education. She wrote her thesis on the correlation between academic and social life for college students. She realized, though, that the stress of managing staff, students, and administration wasn't healthy and, in her opinion, had contributed to causing her cancer.

As soon as she could, Janice resigned from that position, and together with her husband, Mark, moved to Boise, Idaho, where she got certified as a life coach and got her master's degree in Health Sciences in Health Promotion. Today, she is cancer-free and helps people live happier, healthier lives with a focus on community health.

Janice was my role model for facing adversity and choosing a career that brings joy. When she was first diagnosed, it really put things into perspective for me. I thought to myself, *I don't know how much longer I have to live on this planet, and I'm not going to spend another minute miserable and unhappy.*

It was as if the universe was asking, "How many clues do I have to send your way?" It seemed that every time I tried to ignore the signs and push against what I knew deep down was right, the universe would conspire to bring me back to where I was meant to be. The message was clear: it was time to stop resisting and start embracing my new path.

When I graduated from massage school in the spring of 2006, I launched my practice. My plan then was to do massage in the evenings and on weekends until my practice grew enough to support me quitting my IT job.

Shortly after graduating, I learned that one of my instructors, Kevin, was moving out of state, and he recommended to the owner of Bodymechanics that I be brought on as an assistant instructor so that I could be trained before he moved away. Just a few weeks after graduation, I started teaching at the school I'd graduated from. I hadn't considered becoming an instructor, but when Kevin suggested it, I jumped at the opportunity. It was time to give myself fully to massage therapy with a newfound sense of purpose and determination to live life on my terms.

Being able to teach at the school that profoundly changed my life and shaped my future was an incredible opportunity. I found joy and meaning in connecting with students and helping them grow and learn in the same ways that I had. I taught at Bodymechanics for three-and-a-half years, during which I developed my own teaching style and began to see the impact I was having on my students' lives. It was a privilege to be a part of shaping the next generation of massage therapists.

Had I not listened to that alarm clock moment in 2004, had I not started on the path to run that first marathon, I would still be working at a job that was unfulfilling. Or, possibly, I'd be dead from the stress.

Steve Jobs once said, "You can't connect the dots looking forward; you can only connect them looking backward. So you have to trust that the dots will somehow connect in your future." I believe this to be true. You have to trust those gut feelings, those cosmic alarm clock moments, that voice telling you to go for it.

Even if you can't see the whole picture, listen to the guidance you're getting. We all deserve to live a life that's fulfilling, one that lights us up and allows us to share our true selves with the world.

Starting out on this path, I didn't have any direction besides just running. But that running brought me to my first massage therapy session. And that massage session sparked a vision for a future that was bigger than my past.

It was challenging to consider leaving my full-time job. Arlin and I had many conversations about what it would look like and how I would earn as much money as I had been in IT. I remember telling him that if I didn't take the opportunity, massage would always be on the side. I'd always be working two jobs, and I would always be exhausted. He supported me in quitting my job and launching my business. I fully committed to making the change, to aligning myself with that vision. I was more than ready to forge my own path and never have another boss ever again.

When I quit my IT job, I gave three months' notice and called it a "transition from full-time employment." I dropped down to working three days a week on Mondays, Wednesdays, and Fridays. I had plenty of paid time off, so I was still getting paid for full-time work. This meant that the other two days of the week, Tuesdays and Thursdays, I could focus solely on teaching at the massage school and massaging clients. This provided an opportunity to build my practice while still having the safety net of full-time pay, and it provided my employer time to find and train my replacement.

Three months later, I was on my own. I relied 100 percent on my skills, abilities, and determination to create my own path in the world. I went all in on myself. Being self-employed in those first few months was both exhilarating and terrifying. I navigated the challenges of building a business from scratch, learning to be a teacher, and adjusting my life to a new way of working and a new schedule.

At first, I dealt with a constant low level of fear that I'd made the wrong decision. But with each small success, I gained more confidence in my abilities and felt more certain that this was the right path for me. I poured all of my energy and focus into my work, determined to make it a success. Slowly but surely, my efforts paid off.

My dots connected when I realized that I had become numb from fear. Though it began as a form of protection from the bad things that I'd experienced, the numbness was bleeding into the good things as well. I wasn't enjoying life. I wasn't even living life.

I needed to un-numb myself.

That moment I decided to answer the subconscious call to go running without questioning it was the moment I started to feel again. I was drifting through life, accepting whatever came my way instead of being an active participant in creating opportunities and finding true joy. This is why Become Un-Numb is the first of my Five Pillars for Life; without it, nothing else is accessible.

I didn't realize it at the time, but taking on that IT job was the original catalyst I needed to challenge myself. Because I'd built that career from nothing, I knew I was capable of doing it again. That led me to running the marathon, which led me to that first massage, which led me to a new, more fulfilling career.

At the end of my first year in practice, I had earned more in my new career using my own hands and my own mind than I ever had as an IT director. I was healthier. I was incredibly happy. I was thriving. I took a risk on myself, and though it was challenging in the beginning, it was the best thing I could have ever done for me.

Now I was living to live, not living to die.

PILLAR #2

— Movement Is Life —

ONE

Massage has been around for thousands of years, with some of the earliest textual evidence dating back to around 3000 BCE. Throughout the centuries, it has been variously accepted and persecuted, always fighting to be recognized as a valid part of healthcare. But massage remains the most instinctive and natural thing we do for ourselves when we are sore. Bump your leg and I can guarantee that the first thing you'll do is reach for it and rub the pain point.

Before I received my first massage, I was a skeptic about the health benefits of massage therapy, mostly because I hadn't thought of massage at all. This likely stemmed from being very shy and antitouch growing up. My family didn't really display affection when I was young, and I didn't see a lot of physical contact between my parents. If I had to guess, I became introverted around new people because of how often we moved around as kids, leading to a shyness that lingered until I got to know someone. Like most people, I went to the doctor when needed, which wasn't often. My dad was a pharmacist and would bring home medicine if necessary. I wasn't exposed to natural therapies. I was raised in a very Western medicine family.

The truth is that massage therapy changes people's lives. I see it every day. It happened to me when I received my first massage.

I had an experience with my dad that best describes this belief. One year he was scheduled for a knee replacement surgery, and walking was a painful chore. At the time, he lived on the other side of the state of Washington, so we didn't see each other often, and I didn't know that his pain had gotten to the level of near immobility until I saw him for Thanksgiving.

After dinner, I took him to my massage office and proceeded to stretch his legs and hips. When I finished, he stood up and exclaimed, "Look at this! I can walk without pain." He followed it up with, "But I don't get it. It was just massage." He was wavering between joy and confusion like it were a battle of good versus evil in his very traditional-healthcare mind. It made me so happy to know I helped my dad out of pain, but I was sad that this wasn't a healing modality he'd ever been exposed to despite working for so many years in the healthcare industry.

Many people don't get it until they experience the benefits for themselves. There's also another side that makes it difficult to explain to those who need scientific proof: sometimes massage therapy just works, and we aren't sure why. But it's okay not to have all the answers. Seeing the joy and wonder on clients' faces when they get up from the table feeling so much better is enough for me to know that massage is a crucial, integral part of healing that everyone could benefit from.

TWO

During the 2008 and 2009 recession, Bodymechanics began losing enrollment due to federal funding limitations for vocational students. The regulations imposed new restrictions on the amount of debt that students could take on and required that vocational schools meet certain performance metrics in order to remain eligible for federal funding. Because of these metrics, the owner decided to close the school. This was devastating news, as teaching had become a true passion of mine.

But I had another cosmic alarm clock moment: What if I could do something to keep the school going rather than watching it become another victim of the economy?

After negotiating, I bought Bodymechanics in 2010. It was a risky move, and there were many times when I doubted whether I had made the right decision. But as I poured my heart and soul into transforming the school into the kind of institution I wanted, those doubts began to fade away.

I set about learning how to manage a school, committing to this next phase in my growth journey. I began to read management, business, and self-help books, and attend conferences on leadership, business, marketing, and personal development. My goal was to create an environment that fostered innovation, creativity, and student success. I knew that to push through the glass ceiling and make my business a success, I had to grow as a leader. I also made a conscious effort to learn my strengths and weaknesses. It was a challenging and sometimes humbling process, but I remained committed to my goal of becoming the best possible leader for my school.

Early classes at my school saw class sizes between six and ten students. The program took about eight months to complete and was six hundred hours long. We offered morning and evening classes, and students went to school four days a week, four hours a day. Morning sessions were Tuesday through Friday, and evening classes were Monday through Thursday. Students either attended morning or evening classes, and with staggered starts throughout the year, each cohort was at a different part of the linear training.

Initially, I had four instructors besides myself. I had an anatomy instructor who taught one day a week and a kinesiology instructor who taught just one class a week. I taught business classes as well as specialized medical massage modalities. The final instructor taught most of the Swedish massage techniques. As Bodymechanics grew, I began hiring more.

When I bought the school, I changed the payment terms to allow students to take several years to pay their tuition, bringing their monthly payment down to less than that of a traditional car payment, around four hundred dollars a month. Many of those students were on payment plans that provided enough monthly recurring revenue so I could pay the bills. As this was on the tail end of the recession, I thought this was a viable strategy to not only grow the school but also sustain it during tough financial times.

Bodymechanics had a website and a phone number, but in 2010, that wouldn't get you very far. There were suddenly so many more ways for people to find things. I realized that if I wanted potential students to find the school, I had to branch out. I started a business page on Facebook and later Instagram, but I felt I needed to learn these platforms on a deeper level if I wanted to use them as a tool to engage with potential students.

When a friend suggested I attend a weekend marketing conference in California, I jumped on it. I trusted my friend and valued his opinion, and I knew I needed to learn more about marketing. He told me that the guy putting on the conference, Bedros Keuilian, was a "marketing genius," so I bought my ticket to join. The conference was called Fitness Business Summit, and walking in, I saw over four hundred attendees. My first thought was, *This guy* is *a genius if he got four hundred people here!*

Over the course of the weekend, I heard amazing speakers. Garrett Gunderson, a finance expert, spoke about his *New York Times* bestselling book *Killing Sacred Cows*. Jay Abraham, a top executive coach and marketing strategist, spoke about marketing and his book *Getting Everything You Can Out of Everything You've Got.*

I was also introduced to a concept called a *mastermind*. This is a group of like-minded business professionals who come together for peer support. Collaboratively, they tap into their collective wisdom with a goal of accelerating learning and progress for each of their businesses. Key elements of a mastermind are learning, accountability, and a sense of community and support, all of which could help me on my growth journey. Over the course of the weekend, members of the 7 Figure Mastermind, which was led by Bedros, shared their successes from the stage. I was in awe of the idea of getting support from people who were on a similar track as me and who wanted my business to succeed as much as I did.

When presented with the opportunity to join the mastermind, I didn't hesitate. Over the next year, our group met quarterly to discuss goals and challenges, and I received invaluable feedback, tips, and ideas. As the only massage school owner in the group, I was a bit of an anomaly. The rest of the group owned gyms or ran fitness boot camp classes. What I found during each mastermind weekend was that there were strategies used in the fitness world that would help me grow my massage school. For example, one concept I learned about was how to foster group mentality in purchasing decisions, a tactic that is commonly used in the fitness world. Often, free trainings are offered to bring in a lot of interested fitness members, ranging from nutrition classes to coaching on how to lift properly. When someone comes to a free training or discussion, the sell is easier if they've met someone who will be doing the training program with them.

I took this concept and offered group information sessions to interested students twice a month. We would have between five and fifteen people attend these information sessions, and they could listen to questions others had and hear my answers. This increased the number of students who applied to my school. It also helped me work more efficiently. Instead of meeting with students every hour who would ask the same question, I was able to answer the question just one time.

Each mastermind session offered different ideas that I was able to mold to fit my business. I met one of my good friends, Adrian, who was from Ottawa, Canada, through the mastermind. We have remained friends and still talk throughout the year about different business strategies.

I also came up with the idea of adding some fitness offerings to my business, and with the encouragement of my mastermind group, I bought a license to use the Fit Body Boot Camp system. Today, Fit Body Boot Camp is a fitness franchise dedicated to transformation and designed to offer fitness classes in as little as thirty minutes a day, though the system wasn't as defined when I bought the license. I received training on running a fitness boot camp program and was able to operate the gym as I wanted. Being a lifelong athlete, I loved the idea of bringing fitness classes to my community. I already believed wholeheartedly in movement as a source of healing as well as health, and a fitness training system seemed like the perfect holistic addition to help round out and support what I was already offering through massage therapy.

I bought fitness equipment like dumbbells, kettlebells, and medicine balls and made space for it all at the massage school. I set up a schedule for boot camp classes around the massage school schedule.

For the first several months, I began my day with two boot camp classes at 5:45 a.m. and 6:30 a.m. Anywhere from six to ten boot camp participants would come every morning and work out together, with me leading the classes. Then, after the second boot camp session, I would take down all the fitness equipment and set up the massage school, which could be rows of massage tables or a lecture table with chairs depending on what kind of class we were doing that day.

I'd go home, shower, eat breakfast, and then either go back to Bodymechanics to teach or head to my professional clinic to massage my clients. It was exhausting, but I loved every minute of every day. I finally felt like I was where I was meant to be, doing what I was meant to be doing, and it infused so much energy and joy into my work despite the challenges.

Plus, things started taking off. I was soon able to hire two trainers for the boot camp so that I wouldn't have to get up so early in the mornings and could focus on the massage school.

I was leasing two office buildings—one for the professional clinic where I had five treatment rooms and the other for the massage school and boot camp. It felt disjointed and chaotic, as staff were going back and forth between the two buildings, but I didn't think there were any other options.

While reading Garrett Gunderson's book *Killing Sacred Cows*, though, I had an epiphany. Gunderson describes a *sacred cow* as an idea or belief that is held in high esteem in society. He was specifically talking about traditional retirement plans in the US where people put money into 401(k)s or IRAs and live for the someday rather than now, which didn't really have anything to do with my situation. But the real meat of the book was his description of scarcity and abundance mindsets and how using your money today to help you achieve the life you want is more desirable than the someday mentality.

A light—or more like a siren—was going off in my brain.

There I was with two buildings and a process that was very inefficient. I was living in a scarcity mindset, making do with what I had because I thought saving whatever money I could was the smart plan. But the truth was that my businesses were taking off, and I was holding them back because of my scarcity-based fear. What if I focused on abundance? On funneling the money I did have back into the business to help it grow rather than just stay static? I had a new goal: to find a new building to house the massage school, professional massage clinic, and fitness boot camp all in one place. And I found it. The cherry on top? It was just a mile and a half from my home in Tumwater, Washington.

I worked with Robert, a wonderful realtor who helped me through the process, which included updating my business plan and talking to banks. Over the course of several weeks, I met with three different banks, all of which said no to my commercial loan of almost a million dollars, explaining that my business was too new and thus too risky. I was passionate about the potential for this building, quick on my feet to answer questions, and full of energy, but the loan officers just sat behind their laminate desks and didn't say much. This was on the heels of the recession, and banks were stingier about giving loans for what could be deemed risky business ventures.

After that third no, I went home and said to myself, *The universe will provide when the time is right.* I wasn't upset or worried. I just knew that I was meant to own that building and that it would happen when it was meant to happen.

I read another impactful book called *Think and Grow Rich* by Napoleon Hill. Hill interviewed wealthy people who'd lived through the Depression about how they kept or gained their wealth, and the book shares their secrets. One of the strategies mentioned was a mastermind group—and, well, I had already joined one of those! It was a clue that I was on the right path.

After reading the book, I felt even more sure that I could actualize what I needed. I lay in bed every night saying *I need money, I need money, I need money* over and over in my head. I would say these words one hundred times before going to sleep, and I would repeat them again first thing every morning when I woke up. The idea behind this kind of repeated affirmation, which came from *Think and Grow Rich*, is that there is someone in the universe who has a desire to help you, and when the message is heard, the universe will bring you together.

Four months after being turned down by the banks, the universe provided my angel in the form of Duane Stephens.

Robert called me out of the blue one day. "There's been a development on the building you're interested in," he told me.

The building now had a new owner, someone with funds to help whoever bought it with the purchase and design buildout for their business. Robert set up a meeting with the owner, Duane, and his realtor.

My first thought upon seeing Duane, who was in his late seventies, was *He looks like my dad!* I told myself that this was going to be just like sharing my plans in a conversation with my dad. With that relaxed mindset, I went into the meeting, confident that he would see the benefit of my vision and want to support me, just like my dad would.

I told him about the hardships I'd been through with the deaths in my family—losing three family members in seven years. I told him why I became a massage therapist, how I believed this career saved my life, and that I'd bought Bodymechanics to save it when the previous owner closed it down. I shared that part of my dream was to teach others how to follow their dreams too.

When I was finished telling my story, Duane said the eight most impactful words I had ever heard: "Well, I think we can make something work." He explained that he had received help in his life when he needed it, and now he was in a position to pay it forward.

Inside I was jumping up and down and screaming in excitement. Outside I remained cool, nodding my head. At the end of the meeting, Robert and I walked out, and he said, "I think you did it, kid!" I was positive there was a higher power at work, but I also felt so justified that my confident belief and patience had paid off.

Duane and I signed a private multiyear contract on December 3, 2012, which gave me ample time to build my business so that I could refinance it with a bank at some point in the future. He financed the buildout of the building to create space for the massage school, the fitness facility, and the professional clinic, with room for seven professionals to rent space from me, three administrative offices, and a kitchen.

Watching the space take shape during the buildout phase was amazing. My daughters, staff, and I would stop by weekly to witness the massive changes. To see the parking lot full of work trucks on a Sunday as they worked to complete the buildout as soon as they could made me so happy.

Though this was an exciting time for me, it also brought some new revelations to light about my marriage. When I graduated from massage school, Arlin was supportive. He helped me craft the letter that I gave to my employer, which provided a three-month phaseout from working in IT. He supported my business as it grew for the first couple of years. But he worked for Boeing and was home every day by early afternoon, and I was often working until after ten at night if I was teaching the evening class, focused on growing my business. This meant that our time at home didn't often overlap.

Figuring out when things changed in our marriage is hard—it wasn't any one thing that I can put my finger on. If I had to point to anything, it seems that this lack of time together could be it. Arlin wanted to spend time with me, and I was busy building something that felt very impactful to me. It wasn't just me that the business was supporting, as by this point Hayley and Ashleigh were working for me as well. I felt proud to be able to offer our kids jobs.

When I bought the building, I shared everything with Arlin. I remember many weekend lunches where I would share the process, tell him where we were in the buildout and what funds I had to come up with along the way to close the deal. For some reason, he didn't show much interest in the building. One day when we were driving home from lunch, I asked him if he wanted to see the space. He agreed, so we stopped in and saw the crew working hard. I pointed out the different rooms and told him about the purpose for each. He talked with the workers, and the visit was going smoothly.

Duane and his sweet wife, Irene, were on-site as well that day. They invited us to stop by their office for a chat and a beer later, so we did. At one point, Irene—who was and continued to be one of my staunchest supporters over the years—looked at my husband and asked, "Aren't you so proud of your wife?"

Arlin said nothing. Didn't crack a joke. Didn't say yes or no. Nothing.

I was so embarrassed that my husband didn't express pride in what I was creating. I was also sad. Did he not care about my vision? Did he not understand the level of commitment I had to building this business? That was the beginning of the end of our marriage.

We moved in December 2012 when the building was completed. Eight months later, I told my husband I wanted a divorce.

The divorce was emotionally painful, yet it was done with the least amount of trauma possible. Neither of us wanted the divorce to be contentious, and we didn't want to pay lawyers thousands of dollars arguing over belongings, like our house. We agreed that I would keep the house, and he would move out. He would keep his retirement funds. We would split the bills evenly. The lawyer called it a "collaborative divorce." We did the work, and she filed the papers.

I was married for twenty-three years, which was probably five years longer than I should have been. We raised two kids together and now share seven grandkids. Yet, when it mattered, I felt Arlin didn't support me once I began my entrepreneurial growth journey. It wasn't a bad marriage; it just wasn't right for me anymore.

No one ever got anywhere in this world by being content.

My dad wrote these words to me in a card while I was going through my divorce, and when I read them, they brought tears to my eyes. To feel his love and support through my biggest life challenges meant the world to me.

My dad lived those words every day.

My parents had been married for forty-one years when my mom passed away, and they were my role models for what marriage should look like. Growing up, I believed that you stayed married even if there were challenges, and I'd seen my parents face those challenges and come out better on the other side. But that didn't feel right for my relationship. When I decided to get a divorce, I hesitated to tell my dad because I didn't want to disappoint him. I sure gave him a lot of power in my head for all those years, because when I told him, he said he was sorry to hear about it, and that was the end of the discussion. I didn't disappoint him at all.

We look to our parents for help and support for as long as we can; they are usually good at recommending a plumber or can be someone to help with childcare. I'm so grateful for everything my parents gave me over the years. But some problems are beyond their abilities, and it becomes necessary to build a bigger network of support. In times of great distress, there is an opportunity to evaluate those around you and decide if they are helping or hurting your efforts to thrive.

My healing journey felt massive. I had to keep my business going—my kids, grandkids, students, and staff were all relying on me. I had bills to pay, personally and professionally.

I'm thankful that I had so much support from my family, friends, coworkers, and students during my divorce. They lifted me emotionally, mentally, and even financially when I was down. They encouraged me to keep going when I struggled.

THREE

I once had to cut ties with a long-term friend and employee when it became obvious that keeping him around me and my business was detrimental. It was something I kept putting off, because I knew it would be uncomfortable to say goodbye. But it was becoming damaging to keep him around just to avoid that difficult conversation.

I told my lawyer, "I think I need to have a work divorce." Getting help and advice from her helped me to see that I wasn't wrong. The relationship was no longer serving me or my business and in fact may have caused irreparable harm had I allowed it to continue.

Similar to when I went through my actual divorce, I learned an important lesson in my development as a leader during this time. I needed to discover my strengths and weaknesses, and I needed to learn boundaries. One weakness I discovered is that I tend to believe everything someone tells me. My kids tell me that all the time, saying, "Mom, people always tell you what you want to hear and then say the opposite to everyone else."

The situation with this person was that he was no longer content in his role at Bodymechanics. I learned that he was talking poorly about me, my kids, and the school to my students, and he was doing it to make himself look better. This caused the students to have negative feelings toward my school and me, and it eroded the school's credibility. The students could feel the disharmony, and unfortunately, many students had a less than positive experience at my school at the time.

I thought our working relationship had been a good one. He told me what I wanted to hear, but Hayley had overheard him talking badly about the school and me to his massage clients on more than one occasion. Hayley and Ashleigh both told me what he was saying, but I had a hard time believing it. If he was so upset, surely he would talk to me about it, right?

It wasn't until a former student told me what he was saying about my kids and me that I took action and talked to my lawyer about the "work divorce." I saw this as a mirror of my marriage and recognized that I kept him around longer than I should have, just like I had with Arlin. I thought I had to stick it out, to make it work no matter what. But the truth is that if relationships aren't right for you, your business, or your life, you don't have to keep them around. Even if it hurts to let them go.

There's an old story of a person walking on a pier in Alaska who saw a bucket filled with crabs. He observed a crab climbing the side and trying to skuttle away. He pointed this out to the fisherman, warning him of the escaping crab. The fisherman was not worried, saying, "It's okay—watch what happens."

The man watched as the crab reached the top of the bucket. It was almost at the edge when the other crabs below, also scrambling to escape, grabbed its legs and pulled it back down. All the crabs were only in it for themselves, which meant none of them would ever succeed at escaping.

Though firing someone is never easy, a good company culture is dependent on every member believing in it and working toward it. Even one drop of poison ruins the whole pot of milk, as the saying goes. I now have a person who serves as a buffer between my employees and me and handles the difficult conversations after recognizing I don't handle them well, and I can't be in a position again that might harm my business due to my desire to take everyone at face value. I've also learned to trust my daughters a lot more in their leadership roles at the school. They're smart and savvy leaders.

I saw my business and relationships with staff and students thrive after cutting ties with the person who did not support us. Emotionally, it's hard to let go, but if you're in a situation in your professional life where the relationship is not helping you thrive, it's time to say goodbye.

During a hurricane, it's hard to see through the storm. But afterward, when you can sit in silence and think of who supported you and who didn't, it becomes easier to recognize whom you want to spend your time with. For me and my growth, it started with the people around me who supported me. The smallest things can lift us up—a kind word, a show of support, nonjudgmental good advice, and a positive attitude. All of these are easy to do and don't cost any money.

It dawned on me that this same concept held true in my circle of friends and family. People who did not support me through my challenges or were creating more stress, more headaches, and more drama when I interacted with them could not be allowed to rule my life.

FOUR

When asked if I wanted to do an extreme mud run in October 2013, I jumped at the opportunity. I had done some small, community-based mud runs with friends and family and enjoyed them. In the midst of my divorce, I thought that taking it up a notch would be a good challenge for me.

I also thought competing in the event would help me feel more alive. I had already lost half of my family to death, and my marriage was ending. I was ready for something new that I could feel good about succeeding at.

Being a lifelong athlete, I felt I could handle the event. I'd played sports year-round for much of my life and was still consistently doing boot camp classes too. Doing a mud run, I thought, would be a fun way to spend a day.

There is no real training for a mud run. You're running in the mud, climbing over or under obstacles. I watched some videos on YouTube prior to the event and thought I could handle it okay. I didn't think it was risky—and even if it were, I wasn't afraid. I enjoyed a physical challenge.

That day, October 6, 2013, ended with me having to decide if amputating my pinkie finger was better than doctors trying to reattach the nerves, muscles, and skin.

When the specialist hand surgeon said those words to me—"If it were me, I would say, 'Take the finger'"—I just sunk down and said, "I guess, take the finger."

I felt so defeated.

I pulled the sheet and blanket over my head and just let the doctor do what he had to do.

My hand was cleaned and prepared.

The rest of me was a filthy mess. I was covered in mud from head to toe. My friends were there with me and held my other hand.

I heard a snip. Followed by another snip.

I was crying and in shock at what was happening to me. The doctor described what he was doing, but I couldn't look. He cut the fifth metacarpal bone down to a stump. It was cut low enough that he could pull the skin over the bone and stitch it together.

My hand was bandaged up, and they prepared to discharge me from the hospital.

I thought, *They're sending me home an hour after an amputation? I've just suffered a major trauma and they're sending me home?!*

My friend brought in the dry, clean clothes I'd prepared for after the mud run, and I changed. Just that bit of movement brought on extreme pain, and I was given another shot of hydromorphone. I felt another *whoosh* sweep through my body.

I sat in the front passenger seat on the drive home, and every time I moved I felt intensely nauseated. If I just sat perfectly still, I was okay.

When we got to my home, I could barely stand without feeling like I was going to pass out. My soon-to-be-ex-husband had to give me a shower and clean the mud off me.

Later that evening, Hayley and her daughter came over, and Mackenzie, who was five at the time, took one look at my hand and exclaimed, "Grandma! How are you going to count to five?!" It was so sweet, and it made me laugh.

The first week after the accident was a blur. I was in a lot of pain—physically, emotionally, and mentally.

Calling my dad to tell him was one of the hardest things I had ever done—but it was one thousand times better than imagining him getting a call saying that I had died, so there was that.

I started to piece together what had happened in the hospital. I had been in such shock and pain, and then under the effect of the drug, so it felt like a strange, hazy dream. I had a lot of pain and bruising in my forearm. I knew that the doctor had described the tissue that was ripped off my hand as eight or nine inches long, and I realized that there was deeper damage in my arm than I had imagined.

The next morning, I reached out to a friend who worked for a local orthopedic clinic. She was able to get me an appointment the next day with the best hand surgeon in the area.

I arrived for my appointment and filled out the paperwork as best as I could with my nondominant hand. It looked like a child filled in my medical history.

I was taken back to the exam room, and when the nurse started taking off my dressing, I began to cry. I had told her I wasn't ready to look at my hand, but she took off the dressing anyway. I'm sure it was standard for her to look at that sort of trauma, but it wasn't for me. I wasn't prepared for what I saw on my hand.

I saw a nub of a finger.

I saw dried blood.

I saw black stitches.

I saw a grossly swollen and distorted hand.

She covered the hand, and I waited for the doctor.

Dr. Gregory Byrd was the best doctor I could have imagined for my hand trauma. He was gentle and kind. He examined my hand and listened as I described the injury and what the emergency room doctor had told me.

Dr. Byrd told me that the muscle that had been ripped off was called the flexor digitorum profundus (FDP). This muscle has a large tendon that attaches to each fingertip and up to the muscle in the middle of the forearm. This muscle flexes the fingers and helps with wrist flexion. This means it is necessary for making a fist or any action that involves gripping.

If you make a fist and then flex each curled finger in turn—from pinky to index finger and back—you can see the tendons in your wrist dance. If you put your other hand on the middle of your forearm and do these same actions, you will feel the muscle contracting in your arm. That's the FDP. I had ripped the pinky portion of this tendon out of my arm up to that mid-forearm muscle.

Dr. Byrd described the importance of this muscle to me in a way I hadn't thought of before. 50 percent of your grip strength comes from your pinky and ring fingers, and I had ripped off 50 percent of that needed strength. The best-case scenario was that my dominant hand would be half as strong as it had been.

We talked about me being a massage therapist and the fact that I use my hands every day to do my job—from massaging clients to demonstrating techniques for students. I expressed concern about my hand, wondering if this injury would affect me professionally.

Dr. Byrd told me that client care could be affected by a stump. I asked why, and he said that the muscles that controlled the finger were ripped out. Dr. Byrd helped me to understand that if I were to leave the stump on my hand that (a) it would be very noticeable and (b) I wouldn't be able to move it. There was a chance it could get "stuck" on a client—say under a scapula—and cause me more pain and discomfort. Not to mention the fact that this would be a gross thing to experience.

I can't say enough how much I appreciate Dr. Byrd's explanation and gentle understanding of what I was experiencing, and how he recognized and thought through the impact on my career.

He told me about a surgery he could perform called a ray resection, where he would cut the metacarpal bone down to about a quarter inch in my hand, tuck the musculature that previously attached to the bone inside, along with the remaining nerve, and stitch me up.

Having this surgery would make it less obvious to the casual observer that I was missing a finger, and it would alleviate the stump that could get stuck under a client's scapula—or other bones.

"How many of these surgeries do you do?" I asked.

"About six a year," he responded.

Six a year! That seemed like a lot of missing digits in my town.

I asked if there was an outcome potential that I should be aware of if I proceeded with the surgery. He told me that the biggest risk was for a neuroma (pain due to the disruption of nerve cell growth) at the site of the nerve injury. But he assured me that if he did his job right, it shouldn't be a problem.

When it comes time to make a decision, I move pretty quick. There's no reason to sit and think about something like this, as it just makes it harder and harder to decide. Your mind starts playing tricks on you, and you'll think about everything that could go wrong. So I said yes to the surgery.

One week later, I was having a ray resection of the fifth digit on my right hand, ready or not. I got on the operating table, and the nurse asked me what happened to my hand as the doctor was administering anesthesia. She probably heard me say five words before I was out for the count.

Surgery was over in about an hour.

When you have surgery on your hand, they give you a nerve block that makes your whole arm useless for several hours. The surgery was successful, and they sent me home, telling me, "Don't try to use your arm in the middle of the night!"

I will tell you this—when they tell you to not try it out, listen to them.

I went home and took a nap on the couch. When I woke up, I started feeling my hand again. It was similar to the feeling you have when a limb falls asleep. You feel the tingling when it's waking up, and you start to move the limb, but it's kind of weird and doesn't quite respond right.

I took oxycodone for the pain when I went to bed later that night. In the middle of the night, I felt my hand even more. I used my other hand to raise my right arm toward the ceiling and gently moved it around. I looked to my left and reached for my phone on the bed with my left hand—and about killed myself as my still-waking-up right arm went dead and collapsed. When I describe this today, I say, "My quick-as-a-cat reflexes caught my arm before I karate chopped myself."

You would think I learned my lesson.

Nope.

I tried it again later in the night with the same results.

Days went by in a blur. I returned to the office when I was up for it—which was pretty quickly. It's hard to stay home long when you have a doer personality.

All of my massage appointments had to be canceled, as I was operating one-handed while I healed. But being around my kids, my staff, and the students made me feel a lot better than sitting at home on the couch crying about my finger.

A week after surgery, I went to my first occupational therapy appointment. I was to be fitted for a splint. The therapist asked me if I wanted to go to a private room to have the dressing removed.

"No, I'm okay."

"Are you sure you don't want a private room?" she asked.

"No, really, I'm okay," I said.

"I'm going to go see if a private room is available," she responded.

She found a room and took me in and began to remove the dressing. I started crying when I saw my hand. Though I knew my finger was gone, seeing it (or, rather, *not* seeing it) was completely different. It still makes me emotional today. I had stitches wrapped from the backside of my hand to the top of where the finger should have been and then back around to the palm side of my hand.

My hand was grossly swollen. I just cried silently. I was glad she got me a private room; I guess she really understood how I would respond.

I asked if the dressing would be replaced after treatment, and she said that it was my choice. I asked her to redo the dressing.

"I just don't feel comfortable yet with my hand unwrapped," I said, the tears still flowing down my cheeks.

"It's okay," she said. "You earned the right to have it wrapped."

I went to occupational therapy a couple of times a week after that and worked on improving my range of motion. I couldn't make a fist without pain. I couldn't extend my ring finger fully without pain. I also had strange nerve sensations.

One night, I used my right hand to turn on the water in the kitchen and felt a bolt of pain so bad it made me call out. I shook my hand. It was shocking how much it hurt. Hayley was in the living room and asked what had happened. I didn't know. I had not put my hand in the water—just turned on the faucet. But somehow that had caused a jolt of pain.

Any type of vibration also caused a lot of nerve pain for a very long time—something I called nerve zingers. This would be from simple things like pushing the grocery cart out to the car across the rough pavement or gripping the steering wheel when I drove. I would scream out *FUCK* in the car because of the pain if I had to drive more than a few miles.

One day in therapy, I was given a torture device to try to force my ring finger to straighten. In the middle was a hard piece of plastic that would sit on top of the middle knuckle of my ring finger. The underside was counterbracing on the tip and base of the finger, and the spring would try to force the finger straight. I couldn't handle that pain for more than ten seconds without screaming *FUCK*.

Treatment was also filled with ultrasound and grip-strengthening activities. Sometimes they would do things that made my fingers dance uncontrollably, and I would crack up. Every time I went in, they would ask me, "What should we do today?" That question frustrated me so much. The response in my head was always, *I don't know; I've never lost a finger before.*

On October 29, my stitches were removed. Dr. Byrd asked if I was happy with the outcome, and I told him I was, and that he'd done a fantastic job. But I was still sad, mourning what I no longer had.

In the next several months, I noticed things that were difficult for me to do. This included: anything that involved ulnar deviation (side bending) of my wrist, like push-ups; any pressure on my palm from lifting or holding something; holding a weightlifting bar; writing; holding my granddaughter; riding my bike; shaking hands with a tight-gripper; massaging more than one client per day;

scraping change off a counter; and so many other small things that I'd never thought to be grateful for previously.

At my last appointment with Dr. Byrd, I gave him a card thanking him for his skill with my hand. He was right that most people did not notice my missing finger unless I pointed it out. If I'd had the stump there, everyone would notice it. Even still, I found it difficult at first to show my hand to people, always wary of how they'd react.

Now, the fact that most people don't notice my missing finger creates an interesting mind game for me. Losing the finger and all the pain it caused feels massive to me. I get very emotional when I consider how much I have been through physically, mentally, emotionally, and financially since that fateful day. But it feels like an invisible trauma, because most people aren't aware of it. I don't want it to be noticed, yet I need validation about how much I've been through and how much I have overcome. Like I said, it's a mind game.

I've also gained a lot of empathy for people who have chronic pain or an illness that is not visible to the naked eye. As the saying goes, you never know what someone is dealing with, so be kind.

FIVE

As I began navigating my healing journey, I found that I was constantly balancing physical, mental, and emotional pain, with each type of discomfort vying for my attention at different times. I'd been through physical therapy before with my knee surgeries, but healing from this trauma was different. With amputation, there is also a mental side and a deep sense of loss. Depending on the day or moment, one form of pain might be more prominent than the others, making it difficult to find balance and stay centered. It was a roller coaster that I just wanted to get off of.

One day about six weeks after the accident, I was taking a walk in my neighborhood. For some reason, the way the trees were moving in the wind caused me to have my first flashback to the day of the injury. I suddenly felt like I was right back in the moment when I lost my finger. I relived the trauma, confusion, and fear. When the flashback ended, I simply thought, *I don't want to have any more flashbacks for the rest of my life—EVER.*

A peer recommended I go see a hypnotherapist named Shuna Morelli, adding that they knew it wasn't for everyone. "You don't have to go down the rabbit hole if you don't want to," they told me. But I was always trying to be open to new and different things, so the idea intrigued me. I decided to schedule an appointment to see what it was all about.

As I walked into Shuna's office, I felt a mix of nervousness and curiosity, unsure of what to expect. She emphasized that the process was collaborative, and I would be in control the entire time. She asked me what my goals were, and I told her I was afraid to have another flashback, and I didn't want to keep experiencing the kind of excruciating pain that caused me to cry out.

Shuna put me at ease right away, explaining that I would be in a relaxed theta brain wave state. Theta brain waves are strongest when meditating or when practicing strong internal focus. This is the state between being awake and asleep. Theta waves help you access your subconscious mind, which lies beneath your rational, thinking mind and is subtly influencing your decisions and perceptions.

Shuna instructed me to lay on her massage table and covered me with blankets and heating pads, which felt very cozy, warm, and safe. With her guidance, I entered a state of deep relaxation and began to explore my inner world in a way that was both profound and empowering. She began the session by asking me to visualize a trusted advisor to go on this journey with. *I don't know what that means*, I thought, but my mind flashed among my kids, my friends, and my peers, and suddenly it landed on my brother, Steve, who had died in 1997.

The image of Steve was so strong that I felt tears fall from my eyes. Shuna asked what we were doing in my visualization, and I answered, "We're playing catch in a field of wildflowers at the base of Mount Rainier." I saw this image very strongly in my mind—and I can still see it.

One of my earliest memories of my brother was of him teaching me to play catch when I was five and he was eleven. The first thing he said to me was, "If you throw like a girl, I'll hit you!" I didn't want to get hit, but I also didn't know what "throwing like a girl" meant. I guess I did okay, because we played catch a lot as I was growing up, and Steve never hit me. Steve and I had never played catch in a field of wildflowers, though.

Steve became my trusted advisor through the hypnotherapy session. Shuna took me on a journey through my body and asked questions about images I saw along the way. When we got to my hand, she asked about the pain and what image I saw.

I blurted, "It's a jack-in-the-box!" I was imagining the kind where you turn the handle to a little tune until the puppet suddenly pops up.

"Do you want to bury the pain?" Shuna asked.

"Yes," I answered. I invited my dad into the scene and visualized him, my brother, and I putting my pain in a box. Then we buried it under a tree in the field of wildflowers at the base of Mount Rainier. This image still makes me tear up today.

"What do you see as the pain leaves your body?" Shuna asked.

"I see a green witch on a broom, flying away."

The last thing she asked me to do was see my hand as strong. In my mind's eye, my hand was a bowling ball.

I was surprised by the instantaneousness of the strange images popping into my mind as she asked me questions throughout the session. But the lessons I took away were immeasurably helpful. Though I didn't discuss the meaning of the images with Shuna, my takeaway was that *I* could control the turning of the handle of the jack-in-the-box. While I didn't feel like I had gone down the rabbit hole, per se, I did feel like I had gained new insights into myself and my life that I wouldn't have discovered otherwise. Since that one session with Shuna, I have never had that intense pain again. I've also never had another flashback.

Working with Shuna opened my eyes to considering alternative solutions for managing and eliminating pain. I increased my chances of finding relief and improving my overall well-being through my willingness to let go of preconceived notions and explore different paths to healing. I know that this is a mindset that will work for everyone, even if the same methods may not. I also found that sharing my experience with others who are struggling with physical pain can be a powerful way to offer support and encouragement. While there is no one-size-fits-all solution to managing physical pain, I believe that by staying open-minded, tenacious, and compassionate, we can all find our way to greater health and well-being.

Occupational therapy continued to be a mainstay throughout my recovery, though it was a strange and sometimes frustrating process. I learned that the nerve zingers I was feeling were actually called phantom pain. Throughout the day, I had sensations of my missing pinky that I couldn't address: itching, stinging, a heavy feeling, and a need to move the finger. The itchiness and stinging were maddening. I had sensations that would make me jump and call out in pain. I would shake my hand to try to relieve the feeling. As I continued to work with my therapist and follow her guidance, the nerve zingers began to decrease in intensity and frequency. The simple act of rubbing my stump across different textures not only helped to calm my nerves but also served as a reminder of the progress I was making in my recovery.

I was emboldened by my success with hypnotherapy to research other kinds of alternative therapies. I read about mirror therapy and asked my occupational therapist if I could try it.

Mirror therapy was pioneered in the 1990s by the neuroscientist V. S. Ramachandran. It is a way to trick the brain out of phantom pain after amputation, involving a simple box-like structure the size of a notebook with a mirror on one side. You could consider the mirror box as the first "virtual reality" system. My therapist would set the mirror box up on a table, and there was an opening for my right arm to go inside. I'd place my left arm on the table opposite the box, seeing its reflection in the mirror. Then I moved my left hand while looking in the mirror. My brain saw the image and interpreted it as the right hand moving—freely and without pain. As I closed and opened my left hand, I watched the image of the hand in the mirror while simulating the movement with my right hand inside the box.

This was a game changer!

Within two minutes, I had full range of motion of my right hand and could make a fist and fully extend my hand without pain. It felt like a miracle.

The mirror box works because it takes into account how the wiring of our brains is separate from our thoughts. Though I knew the finger wasn't there, my brain remembered my hand and finger prior to the injury; it still had neurons for that finger that were confusedly misfiring. This created a bit of a disconnect in my reality. However, by using the mirror, my brain was able to reconnect visual feedback in response to the movement, which helped to restore my image of wholeness in my hand.

My experience was positive and immediate, with long-lasting results. This alternative modality helped my brain adapt to the loss of my finger, and it also helped me recover from traumatic pain— physically, mentally, and emotionally. I learned that to heal from pain, you have to change the brain's perception of it.

But it left me wondering, *Why didn't we start my healing process with this amazing therapy?*

I knew I wasn't the only person suffering from this kind of pain, and what if others out there weren't looking for alternatives like I had been? If I hadn't asked about mirror therapy, my therapist and I would probably have never tried it. This realization was the seed of a new personal mission: I wanted to help millions of people get out of pain.

While I was recovering from the loss of my finger and working toward being able to massage again, I knew that the way I worked would never be exactly the same. I would have to find new ways to effectively massage clients while factoring in my limitation. This was intimidating, and I went through a grieving period, mourning what had been and all that I'd taken for granted when I had the use of all ten fingers.

Before I lost my finger, I was massaging between twenty-five and thirty clients a week. After the amputation, I wasn't able to achieve that level of clients again. I tried to do a massage about six weeks after losing my finger, but it was awkward, and I felt insecure in my arm function. The extensive damage in my forearm caused weakness that couldn't sustain a full massage practice at the same level.

My divorce was finalized two months after my amputation. My now ex-husband moved out a few weeks later. I was truly on my own and had lost my ability to maintain my previously thriving massage practice. Because I had a lot of guilt about getting divorced and didn't want to cause more trauma for myself or my ex, I didn't ask for any support from him. Looking back, I wish I had asked for alimony for at least a year so I could have had time to adjust to my new reality.

Instead, I struggled to find my balance—emotionally, mentally, physically, and financially. My days were spent teaching at Bodymechanics and trying to figure out how to bring in money that was lost alongside my finger. I focused on growing the school and trying to bring in more students. I tried to grow the boot camp and increase membership. I met with potential students and encouraged them to become massage therapists. I started journaling about what I was experiencing as I was rehabbing my life.

SIX

Scientists have begun to consider neuroplasticity as an answer to brain remapping in response to the environment and trauma. Neuroplasticity is the brain's ability to change through growth and reorganization, rewiring itself around trauma or loss to function in new and different ways so we can keep on living. How fabulous is that? Our very brains are wired for change, and to me, that means that we are adaptable in other ways too, capable of changing our minds, our careers, and ourselves. If only we're willing to take a chance, we'll see that we're stronger than we thought.

The way I teach massage has changed over the years. I now incorporate an understanding of neuroplasticity and discuss how my students can foster a mindset for change in their clients. It's common for someone in pain to avoid activities that cause pain. No one wants more pain, especially when they're feeling it all the time. It's exhausting—believe me, I know. But avoidance is based in fear, which, if I've learned anything, is something to get curious about instead of pushing away. Where is that fear coming from? Why is pain so scary?

The type of massage I teach encourages students to be curious about pain patterns and create movement to help the client feel less fearful. Students are taught to observe the client's range of motion, which may be very limited due to injury. We encourage students to use techniques that will help the clients learn that they can move their body without fear.

Unfortunately, our current model of traditional healthcare encourages activity avoidance if there is pain associated with the activity. Injured people are often told by their healthcare provider to not move the injury, and they may be given pain relievers, muscle relaxants, or splints.

Knee pain with running: people are told to stop running.

Elbow pain with tennis: people are told to stop playing tennis.

Carpal tunnel syndrome causing numbness and tingling: people are told to wear a brace to limit movement.

What this does to the person with the injury is cause them great fear about moving the injured body part, which can lead to scar tissue building up, muscle atrophy, and general weakness.

When I hear that a person has been told by their doctor to avoid an activity that brings them joy, I immediately switch gears and lean into creating a mindset for change in the client. I teach students to use positive and encouraging words as they cautiously move the clients' joints, to show patience and slow down so clients learn that movement doesn't have to hurt.

In 1995, ten years before I went to massage school, I completely ruptured my anterior cruciate ligament (ACL), the ligament that connects the thigh to the shin. It required two surgeries in four months. When I was released from post-surgery care, I asked my doctor if I should wear a knee brace when I played any sport, such as softball or running. He said no—he didn't want me to develop a reliance on the brace. This was advanced thinking back in the nineties; I still see people today who, when recovering from injuries, are immediately put in braces and encouraged to avoid activities that cause any pain. For someone recovering from an injury, one of the worst things to do is stop moving, because it locks in the dysfunction and pain. I'm grateful that my doctor told me not to wear a brace after knee surgery.

Since that surgery, I've remained very active, playing softball and soccer for many years. I ran my first marathon nine years after the knee surgery. I ran a second marathon one year after my finger amputation. And I've since run two more full marathons and several half marathons. I ride my bike. I go for long walks. I've never thought about avoiding activities. Instead, I think of movement as an important piece of my self-care.

Using my life experiences in teaching helps my students understand how to work with people who have injuries. We encourage movement and a salutogenic approach to rehabbing an injury, which encourages well-being and movement with a "gonna try" attitude versus avoidance of activity. In other words, we focus on those things that promote a healthy life as opposed to those things that cause disease.

This approach encourages students and massage therapists to be curious about the origins of an injury and ask deeper questions, such as, "Do you remember a time when you didn't have pain?" This creates an opportunity for the client to contemplate the cause of the injury and helps them see the possibility of change.

I've often said that my favorite quote is "Movement is life; stillness is death." Thinking about this statement in the context of brain patterning, it could be said with a twist: "Movement creates less fear; stillness creates weakness and pain." Stillness creates a perpetuating cycle of pain, which in turn causes even less movement. Eventually this will lead to pain pills, surgery, and joint replacement.

Janice now works in healthcare with the US Department of Veteran Affairs (VA) in the Veterans Health Administration division. Recently she told me about a conversation she had with a doctor, asking if they refer veterans for massage therapy. The doctor's response surprised me.

"To massage? No. If we gave a massage to every vet looking for a massage, it would financially ruin the VA."

I'm not sure how the doctor justified this answer. How is massage more financially ruinous than overprescribing opioids that patients become addicted to or expensive exploratory surgeries to find the source of pain?

At Bodymechanics, I work with many veterans who chose to come to massage school because, when they were injured, massage and other complimentary services got them back in action and feeling better. A healthy veteran who has full use of their body is a much better outcome than an opioid-addicted veteran without hope for a fulfilling life.

One of my employees went to massage school to help her veteran husband for this very reason. She was tired of watching him waste away due to his chronic back pain. He had been prescribed narcotics and spent most days laying around and not living a productive life. Since she started massage school and began practicing on him, she says her husband hasn't taken any narcotics. His quality of life has improved by receiving monthly massage and chiropractic adjustments. I just can't see how this type of treatment would financially ruin the VA.

In addition to helping me grow personally, I began taking what I learned in occupational therapy and applying it to my own work as a massage therapist and teacher. One of my biggest lessons was about the mind-body connection.

When I work with my massage clients and students, I incorporate a mindful approach to and communicate with their brain as part of the session. I often suggest to clients and students that they research the mind-body connection and encourage an outside-the-box approach to help eliminate the trauma that is affecting their quality of life.

For example, I'll use and teach a technique called Proprioceptive Neuromuscular Facilitation (PNF) for a client with shoulder pain and loss of range of motion. The client pushes into the therapist to engage the target muscle and holds the contraction for a few seconds. While they are pushing, the therapist instructs the client to take a deep breath, and then, after a moment, tells them to relax with a statement like, "Tell your brain to just let it all go."

As the client releases their breath and the therapist feels the targeted muscle relax, the therapist will stretch the muscle just a little farther and repeat the cycle a few more times. With repeated cycles of movement, the client can feel the increase in range of motion. Their pain begins to dissipate, and they can confidently move again.

The beauty of this approach is that the client loses their fear. When they feel the freedom of movement, they often exclaim, "Look at that!" As massage therapists, we become their partner in freer movement. We are not healers; we are facilitators who unlock and reveal that movement is possible.

Movement is life. It really is. When you think about it, everything about life is movement! And though physical movement is a key component of my life, this also applies to metaphorical movement toward my dreams or goals. Physical movement can even create momentum for other kinds of movement. When I'm feeling frustrated or stuck in a situation, I'll go for a walk or run. You don't get anywhere by standing still, and stagnancy has never offered me any new opportunities.

That's why Movement Is Life is the second of my Five Pillars for Life.

PILLAR #3

— Follow Your Joy —

ONE

Ascending the stairs to my front door, I saw a paper stapled to the doorframe. It was a notice of foreclosure on my home. I ripped it down and quickly went inside, my face heating up as I wondered if anyone had seen it.

I was so embarrassed and shocked. I had no idea that Arlin wasn't paying the mortgage, as he had done for years.

It was February of 2014. I was newly divorced and still recovering from my amputation. Even before pulling that paper off the door, I'd been worried about finances. I was unable to massage for quite some time, and going into the divorce my plan was to support myself using my massage income. Well, that wasn't happening now.

At that time, notices from the bank were still going to my ex-husband. To make things worse, there was not just one but two houses we still owned together. I called the bank the next day and offered to make a payment, but they wouldn't take any payments until all back payments were paid. At that time, we owed close to twenty-five thousand dollars on both houses in back pay.

The physical, emotional, and financial pain I felt every day was exacerbated by finding a foreclosure sign stapled to my home. It felt like my world was falling apart.

It wasn't supposed to be this way. I was supposed to be finding myself, building my business, and stepping into my power. Instead, I suffered what seemed like a career-ending injury, got divorced, and had my house in foreclosure. I had lost my ability to earn an income and pay my personal bills. I felt myself spiraling down the drain of fear and despair.

I also owned a proprietary massage school that was on the verge of growth. When I lost my finger, I also fell behind on paying the business expenses. I fell behind on this mortgage, taxes, and bills as well. Losing my personal massage income was devastating on many fronts. From when I bought the school in 2010 until the day of my injury, my personal massage practice income went into the general operating funds, which helped with payroll, the mortgage, and other bills. I had to borrow money twice to cover payroll. My dad didn't hesitate, asking only, "How much and when do you need it?" The check arrived within two days, and I was able to pay my staff.

To add to the stress, my kids both worked for me and relied on the income the business provided them. Their kids relied on it also. I was supporting three generations.

I was so close to losing everything—my house, my business, my income, all ripped away in the blink of an eye, just like my finger. I felt like I was failing. People kept telling me I was so strong, but inside I was floundering—wondering where I would get the money to pay the bills.

But because of my kids, failure wasn't an option.

When my dad sent me the check to cover payroll, I got some breathing room. One thing I learned is that I need to reach out and ask for help when I need it. I often have a need to figure out everything on my own, but when I ask for help, I always feel relieved.

Bodymechanics was finally growing and close to standing on its own, but still, covering the lost income felt insurmountable. Duane worked with me, and though I fell behind in paying the mortgage for my beautiful new school building, I didn't lose it during the difficult financial times. Duane saw me for me, knew I was doing the best I could, and was so understanding about the situation. If I had traditional financing, I would definitely have lost it all. I'm not sure the school could have continued if that were the case.

Starting a chapter titled "Follow Your Joy" with a story about foreclosure might seem misaligned, but I have found that joy is always the path through pain and struggle. Joy can be little things, like appreciating the raindrops on the window or hearing your child laugh. Joy can be found in vulnerability when you are supported by your community, such as when my dad and Duane supported me. Their belief in me fired up my belief in myself, the belief that what I was doing was important and could bring joy to others.

Duane died a few years later, and I went to his funeral. There were over four hundred people in attendance, and countless people stood up and shared how Duane helped them financially when they needed it most. I count myself among the many people in my community who benefited from Duane's good graces.

TWO

Running the Seattle Marathon in 2004 set in action a pathway of growth and change—it led me to massage therapy and to a new career. After I lost my finger, I decided to run a second marathon, ten years after my first, as a kind of measuring stick of my strength and resiliency. I also wanted to remind myself of where this path began and focus on something just for myself.

As I began training in 2014, I found that the physical challenges were different than they had been with the first marathon. I had to figure out how to train without irritating my missing finger. I had to overcome emotionally challenging days when I worried about finances, two houses in foreclosure, and meeting payroll for my staff and kids. To the best of my ability, I focused each day on what I could do—counting every little step forward as a win—and not what I couldn't do.

Feeling so untethered, I was losing faith in myself and my businesses. While talking about this with one of my mentors one day, I asked, "How do I get myself inspired again?"

"One thing that helps me," he said, "is using social media to talk to myself." What he meant was that he would write inspiring messages to his audience, but really the posts were what he needed to hear. Posting something like "Don't procrastinate when you have big dreams" would inspire someone reading it on Facebook but also serve as a reminder for him not to give up his own dreams.

I was intrigued, and I decided to give it a try, thinking, *Why not?* The stakes were low, and, at a bare minimum, my words might reverberate for other people even if they didn't for me. On days when I was particularly struggling, I started crafting posts with the messages I thought I needed to hear but didn't really believe. Things like, "No matter what you're going through, you're stronger than you think."

This technique was surprisingly successful on several levels. Putting that positive energy out there in the digital world always felt freeing. People would reply to the post, thanking me for motivating them. The energetic and grateful responses boosted my self-esteem and mood—I knew I had a strong, wonderful community around me that only wanted my success. The idea that my words were making a difference in other people's lives gave me a sense of purpose. I also noticed that I started to believe in my posts. I really was stronger than I thought! I would be filled with motivation to keep things moving forward, one step at a time.

I began to see the power of social media not just as a tool for connecting with others or promoting business but also as a way to create a positive impact on the world. The act of reaching out to others and offering support as they worked through their own struggles became a powerful source of healing and connection for me. In helping others, I was also helping myself—what a revelation!

Along with this, I was discovering that I had a passion for writing, and other people seemed to easily connect with my storytelling. I began opening up more and sharing my personal story of loss as well as what I was doing to turn my fear around those losses into strength. I came to see that my struggles and challenges had given me a unique perspective and a gift for empathy that I could use to help others. Through the act of sharing my own journey, I was able to connect with others on a deep and meaningful level and make a real difference in their lives. I continued to use social media as a way to connect with others, and ultimately my journey through hardship led me to a place of greater strength and resilience. I was able to find hope and truly believe in it, even on the darkest days. A new world of possibilities was opening up for me.

This time around, I decided to work with personal trainers to get ready for the marathon, which was immensely helpful in keeping my training on point. I was working out, lifting weights, eating nutritious food, and running. The joy I felt while training came through in my social media posts, and every day, people told me that I was inspiring them. Their encouragement filled my emotional tank.

I chose to run the Rock 'n' Roll Las Vegas, which is held every year on the Sunday before Thanksgiving. My target goal was to run this marathon one hour faster than my first marathon. By the time Thanksgiving rolled around, I was the fittest I had ever been as an adult, and I felt confident, having completed a half-marathon in the summer with a personal record.

The day arrived. My friend, Shelli, was also there, running the half-marathon to my full. Since it was a rock and roll themed marathon, there was a concert before the run. Macklemore played for an hour, and it was so much fun. The concert meant standing on our feet for an hour before running, though. Plus I was used to early morning runs where I'd get up, have a cup of coffee and a glass of water, eat a snack, then go out. For this marathon, I had to figure out what to eat throughout the entire day so I wouldn't feel sluggish when it started at 4:30 p.m.

After the concert, we made our way to the start, which was a bit of a walk. There were over forty-two thousand runners that year, and I was in pen 42, with hundreds of people in each pen. They started a group every ninety seconds. Because I was in a higher pen, I didn't start running until long after 5:00 p.m.

I started out in high spirits. I had trained well for this marathon and was better prepared than I'd been for my first marathon. I was on track for my target goal, and it felt attainable for most of the run. The first half of the run was on the Las Vegas Strip, past all the casinos, flashing lights, and throngs of people watching and cheering. After about ten miles, those running the half-marathon turned to the left and finished on the strip. Those of us running the full marathon continued out into the Nevada desert. About every mile there was a band playing music, and it was festive and certainly entertaining.

That night was very cold. With most marathons that start in the morning, the temperature gets warmer as the hours get later. The Rock 'n' Roll Las Vegas started in the dark, and the weather only got colder with each passing hour. I was glad that I had a warm hat and gloves to wear.

At some point during the marathon, my watch died. I had already made the turn back to the city and knew I was within a few miles of the finish line, but I hadn't seen a mile marker in a while and wasn't sure how much farther I had to go. I stopped and walked with another participant, asking if he knew where we were on the course. He replied that we were at about mile twenty-three, just three miles or so to go.

His name was Charlie, and he looked pretty rough as we walked. I also noticed he was wearing a shirt that read "I pooped today." That was hilarious—if you're a runner, you know.

"How are you doing?" I asked.

"I think my body is shutting down," he replied. Along with that worry, he was afraid he wouldn't be able to finish. The marathon had a time completion requirement, and if he was too slow, a van would come pick him up and he'd never cross the finish line. I decided to stay and help him out.

"Can you run to that light? Can you run to the end of the block?" I kept encouraging him, and we walked together, running when he could. He told me that this was his first marathon, and he'd thought he would finish in about four hours, but because he had started in an earlier pen than mine, he was over five hours already.

He told me he had turned forty that year. He talked about his family and how he had decided to run a marathon to get healthy for them. He kept repeating over and over his fear about being taken off the course and his body shutting down. I stayed with Charlie because I felt his fear and wanted to support his journey—it is so inspiring to me to witness people do things they feel is impossible. If I can be just a small part of helping people achieve their goals, it's all worth it. With about a quarter mile to the finish line, he told me, "Go and finish, I'm okay—I'm going to make it."

While I didn't reach my goal to run one hour faster than my first marathon, I have a picture of me running across the finish line with a big smile on my face. The lady next to me looks miserable. I know that if I hadn't helped Charlie finish his race, I would have met my goal, but the universe took me to him.

At the end, he found me and gave me a big hug as his wife and daughter looked on. It reminded me so much of my first marathon— the struggle in those last few miles and seeing my family at the finish line. He told me, "I'll probably never remember your name, but I'll never forget how you helped me finish."

I've never forgotten his name, though. Helping Charlie finish his marathon was important to me. I wanted him to have that finish with his family for his first marathon too. Training for my first marathon felt like a personal mission I had to accomplish. While I was so proud of my second marathon, I realized afterward that through the training process, the race had become less and less about me. Seeing Charlie's joy and knowing I'd helped him succeed sparked something in me.

My next mission had already been forming, even though I wasn't fully aware of it. All those social media posts that I'd originally written to inspire myself turned out to do something much bigger, and I loved it. I wanted to focus on inspiring others to get excited about their own goals. I wanted to help motivate them into action. It felt so good to see Charlie celebrating with his family, and that was the tipping point for me, the realization that helping others on their personal paths was my true mission.

THREE

Training for the Rock 'n' Roll Las Vegas also set in motion a pathway of growth and change in the form of a new entrepreneur group. Steve was a friend who had reached out to me and told me that I was inspiring him through my social media posts. He invited me to check out a new group he was in called Maverick1000, which is an invitation-only network of entrepreneurs from all over the world. They were holding an event in Vancouver, BC, in February 2015.

I went to the event not having a clear idea what the group was about, thinking I would be checking them out to see if I wanted to join. I introduced myself on the first day and was asked to share something that made me unique. Since no one there knew I'd lost a finger, I introduced myself by saying that I give a "nine-finger massage, because you can't handle all ten" while holding up my hand. The room erupted in laughter. I knew I was in the right place.

Joining Maverick1000 was a massive step in my entrepreneurial journey. I began spending time throughout the year with other members who were on their own big journeys, all focused on changing the world at the highest level. My mind opened to new possibilities, and my plans grew exponentially. Yanik Silver, who founded Maverick1000 along with his cousin Sophia, created truly life-changing events where I was able to meet some amazing leaders from around the world. With each new event or experience, I felt a growing sense of inspiration and a renewed commitment to creating positive change. Each event gave me a fresh perspective and new ideas for how I could contribute to making a difference. I began to see that my own journey of healing and growth was deeply connected to the journeys of others.

The first day of every event always featured a speaker or thought leader. For example, at one event, we met Sara Blakely, the creator of Spanx, and learned how she developed a billion-dollar company with a $5,000 investment from savings.

On the second day of the event, we worked with a charity, learning about their big challenges, such as raising capital and awareness. We would then split into groups to come up with an idea to help them. One such project focused on supporting a group that helped women and children in danger get out of Afghanistan.

Another time, we helped provide safe-drinking water filters in Puerto Rico after Hurricane Maria devastated the island.

The third day of each event always featured a fun activity that we didn't know about until we arrived at the destination. We were told only when to show up, what to wear, and what to bring with us. I learned about stunt car driving in California, boxed with a champion in Detroit, participated in *The Amazing Race* in Buenos Aires (like the TV show), and went zip lining in Canada. For me, these days were always a mix of excitement and fear, that old monster rising within me to worry about everything that could go wrong. But the idea was to let go of the need to control everything in our lives, play like kids, and trust that we would be taken care of—not always easy for entrepreneurs used to being in control of all aspects of their lives.

As a fledgling entrepreneur, I was blown away by the friendships I made and the people I met. The cherry on top was meeting Richard Branson on Necker Island, his private island in the British Virgin Islands. To this day, I pinch myself when remembering that I have traveled to his tropical paradise twice.

That period in my life was a rebirth. I had been to hell, suffering from the deaths in my family, divorcing my husband, losing my finger, and rebounding from devastating financial struggles. Those financial challenges nearly broke me. Finding my voice through journaling and posting about what I was experiencing and having my friends and family tell me that I inspired them propelled me to a new level.

FOUR

In December of 2015, I returned home from a Maverick 1000 trip in Argentina to a voicemail on my phone. It was from a massage therapist friend, Scott, telling me that a massage school in Vancouver, Washington, had closed their doors forever. The school was part of a national chain that was closed by the government for predatory enrollment practices and poor education. There were many schools closed by the federal government during that time, and not only the massage-related ones.

I set up a lunch meeting a few days later with Scott and another massage therapist who practiced in Vancouver. They talked to me about the need for a good massage school there. Though there were several schools across the river in Portland, Oregon, most people from Vancouver didn't want to drive into Portland because of the traffic. They thought that I, as an entrepreneur with a flourishing school, might be interested in taking on this challenge and expanding.

I took about a month to think it over, but once I made the decision to do it, I moved quickly. I wanted to be first in that market to open a school. In February, I found a perfect location to rent, hired and trained instructors with my curriculum, and started advertising for students. The Vancouver campus of Bodymechanics was launched in March 2016. The school space was set up differently than the main campus in Tumwater but was large and spacious with room for growth. From February to March of that year, I was in Vancouver several times a week, setting up the space, buying equipment, meeting with potential students, holding information sessions, and interviewing instructors. In March of 2017, we launched with five brave students taking a chance on my new school—just three months after I'd heard about the opportunity!

During this time, I also joined a new coaching program called Strategic Coach with Dan Sullivan. My friend Adrian Delorey convinced me to join the Toronto chapter for coaching, and I flew to Toronto four times a year for day-long immersive coaching programs. This was a three-year program, and the first year focused on the entrepreneurs themselves.

As part of this journey of self-discovery, I took the Kolbe A Index. This test doesn't measure intelligence or assess personality; it measures your instinct type, and I learned that I was what it called a Quick Start. The four action modes in the Kolbe test are Fact Finder, Follow Thru, Quick Start, and Implementor.

The report from Kolbe stated, "You are uniquely able to take on future-oriented challenges. You lead the way to visionary possibilities and create what others said couldn't be done. You'll say yes before you even know the end of the question—then turn it into a productive adventure." This defined me to a T and helped me see myself more clearly. It's no wonder I opened a new division of my school in three short months!

Understanding myself as a Quick Start also helped me realize *why* I'm always the first to raise my hand to take on a new task when others are unsure or unable to make a rapid decision. I'm often asked by people who are much more averse to risk why I'm okay with taking a chance. Until I took the Kolbe test, I didn't have an answer. Learning that I'm a Quick Start answered so many questions for me and my personality. This fits with how I've always responded to challenges. I'm good at finding solutions. I'm able to discover alternative courses of action. I love brainstorming. I can easily tell stories. And operating in a sense of urgency does not bother me at all.

I also had my daughters take the Kolbe test and learned that Hayley is a very strong Fact Finder—she needs all the answers before she can take action. I used to frustrate Hayley a lot when I would come back from a Maverick1000 event and be excited for new opportunities, and she would ask, "Again?" with a defeated look on her face. It shut me down. What I didn't recognize is how it froze her in her tracks when I was trying to quickly pivot to something new.

Ashleigh, on the other hand, is very much in the middle of all categories and works well with most people. Through learning about our instinct types, we learned to communicate better. I learned to let Hayley know that what I bring home from events are just fun ideas, that nothing is happening ... yet. She learned to ask me if I've documented every possible outcome and the impact on the company before implementing something.

Though I'm quick to jump on and try new things, I also lack follow-through. Starting new things gives me a lot of energy and motivation, but I need a team to help me complete projects and realize my vision. This is where Hayley's strengths come in very handy—she finishes projects, some of them very complex.

I began connecting dots through my life and making sense of how and why I was able to take chances and risks when other people seemed incapable of taking action—even if it meant that they remained miserable and stuck in a job that made them unhappy.

A very long time ago, I raised my hand in a meeting and began my career in IT. I had zero understanding of how a network worked nor anything beyond how to turn on my computer and do my work for the day.

But I raised my hand and learned over time.

Gaining a deeper understanding and learning that my core operating system is that of a Quick Start helped me embrace who I am. I was able to identify my strengths and weaknesses, which meant I was able to harness my strengths more fully and ask for help where I knew I needed it.

Responding to pain—whether physical, mental, emotional, spiritual, or financial, is different for everyone. No one can or should compare their journey to someone else's. We're all on a journey all our own. What I can say is that staying in a place of pain is no way to live.

Life could have broken me. Some days, overwhelmed with grief, pain, fear, and worry, it felt like the trek was too steep, the mountain so tall that I couldn't see the top of it let alone what might be on the other side. But something inside wouldn't allow me to give up. I could have lay on the couch and been depressed, but what purpose would that serve? I could have been negative and blamed a lot of people for my challenges, but again, what purpose would that serve?

Choosing to move forward with a determination to succeed was my best option for success. Being in the mastermind group before losing my finger helped me to see that I wasn't alone, and I wasn't the only person who had experienced challenges. I'd also learned how to keep moving forward and model strategies for others who had gone through hardships.

Finding my family of entrepreneurs helped me feel like I fit in somewhere. Until then, I hadn't known anyone like me who would raise their hand in a meeting and choose to do something different from anything they had done before. I didn't know anyone else who made a split-second decision that radically changed their life. These friends were just as all in on my success as they were on their own. They pushed me, encouraged me, supported me, and cheered me on through both the good and hard times as I've grown.

The third of my Five Pillars for Life, Follow Your Joy, very much arose out of this time in my life. Yes, there was hardship, loss, and, frankly, even terror at times as I contemplated losing everything that I'd built. But joy lit my path. Joy helped me to see that there's always a way through the darkness, always a hand reaching out to you if you only ask for help. I lost so many members of my family, but I learned to connect more closely with those I still had. I also gained a found family—amazing, brilliant, supportive people I never would have connected with if I'd stayed struggling in the dark alone.

Now if I do something, it better bring me joy!

PILLAR #4

— Move the Boat —

ONE

learned one of my favorite journaling activities from my mentor, Yanik. I open my journal to a random blank page in the middle and draw an image of anything that comes into my mind. Then I flip back to the page I'd been writing on before and forget about the drawing. Journaling every day fills up the pages, and I soon discover my previous drawings. I'm always surprised by these images, because even though they are snapshots of where I was, they always connect to the present moment in interesting ways.

Once, I flipped my journal open to a future page and drew an image I see almost every day—Mount Rainier at sunrise. Under my drawing I wrote, "Wake up with a dream."

A few months later, the Maverick1000 group met on the Big Island of Hawaii. The theme of the retreat was Legendary Legacy. The first day, Yanik inspired us with a legacy talk. At the end of the day, Yanik tasked us with a journaling activity called "Legendary

Legacy" where we would spend some alone time pondering what seeds we were planting to create our legacy. But this wouldn't be just any legacy—it would be legendary. What kind of seeds would create that kind of legacy?

Back in my room, I opened my journal to the next page, and there was the image of Mount Rainier at sunrise with "Wake up with a dream" written underneath. I was shocked that this was the page for that day. I went ahead with the activity and wrote what seeds I was planting, which included taking the lessons I've learned from life experiences to continue to push forward, teach, inspire, motivate, engage, give more, connect, innovate, create, and live life to the fullest. I also wrote down that I wanted to cherish time spent with people having deep and interesting conversations. I would wake up with a dream every day.

When I finished writing and stood, there was a knock on my door. My friend Melinda was there, and I shared with her how amazing it was to turn the page and see my drawing with this activity.

She stopped me, saying, "Shari! Look out your window!"

The view outside was of a huge volcano. It matched *exactly* the image I had drawn in my journal months earlier. I was exactly where I was supposed to be!

I had connected the dots from my past—which really started when I woke up in 2004 to the dream of running a marathon, which led to Bodymechanics, which led to my private practice and ultimately owning the massage school I'd graduated from in 2006. I felt whole. I also felt content and full of energy for what the future could bring.

On another trip to Hawaii in December 2021, I attended a retreat on the Big Island with other highly-motivated entrepreneurs led by my friends Eric and Patrick. We stayed at a local resort owned by Eric and his wife, Lori, called Bliss Island Resort.

After several long days of workshops and brainstorming, our group of nine decided to take a canoe ride offshore to see the beautiful view of the island from the ocean. A long drive to the other side of the Big Island brought us to a beach where we saw two canoes: one with a single hull that held five people with an outrigger for balance and the other with two hulls joined by a curved piece of wood that could hold eight people in total.

A couple of people in the group said that the double hull would be more stable and thus safer, so several of us immediately decided to get in that one. I could swim, but I definitely felt way more comfortable in a swimming pool than the open water. In fact, I'd say I have a healthy fear of the ocean and a full respect for the vastness of the water. The safer boat seemed like a good idea to me, especially considering the weather wasn't exactly perfect that day. It had rained earlier and was still a bit windy.

"I don't love the ocean," I told my friend Justin. "I am ready to face my fears head-on, though."

The guide gave us a quick lesson in paddling, explaining how to alternate sides. The person in the front, called the first position, would start to paddle on the left side of the canoe, and everyone behind them would alternate sides: the second position on the right, third position on the left, and fourth position on the right. The guide explained that we would paddle about twenty strokes on the first side, then he would give a call out, and everyone would switch sides.

We hopped in the canoes and got started. Justin took the first position in the double hull, and I took the second position. There were two people behind me, one being the guide. The other hull we were attached to held four more people. We planned to paddle far enough from shore so that we could turn the canoes around to get a great view of the land and the mountains.

We watched the single-hulled canoe paddle out quickly. They moved beyond a large coral rock, turned, and paused a minute. We followed their path. By the time we navigated around the rock, the team in the first canoe had already turned and were halfway back to the shore.

Our double-hulled canoe was now past the coral rock. We were parallel to the shore enjoying the view when suddenly a large wave hit the side of our canoe. It pushed the hull I was in onto the large rock, and we became stuck.

"Are you okay?" Justin asked me, remembering that I wasn't a huge fan of the ocean.

I replied honestly that I felt fine. Looking at our position, I asked, "Can we all just use our paddles to push off the rock?"

"No," the guide replied. "If we wait a minute, another large wave should come, and I can use that to help lift the canoe off the rock."

He proceeded to get out and stand between the two hulls, grabbing the curved wood that joined them. He waited for a wave that would help lift the hull, but the ocean had other plans. Waves pounded at us, pushing us higher onto the massive rock. Now both hulls were stuck. Waves were hitting the outside hull and splashing everyone. The guide did his best to keep us calm while trying to lift the boat off the rock with each wave.

Both hulls started taking on water. I noticed that there were no life jackets aboard.

Patrick, in the first position on the other hull, was telling everyone to remain calm and take deep breaths. He started singing a song while he scooped out water with his paddle. Despite my growing apprehension as the situation felt more and more dire, I couldn't help but laugh at Patrick. He broke the tension and helped us all back off from our fear. Watching Patrick singing while scooping water will forever be etched in my mind as one of the funniest damned things I have ever seen.

Meanwhile, Bethany, who was also in the other hull, had noticed a crack forming in the bottom, and George was using a milk jug to scoop out water. It was pretty chaotic as the waves were crashing, water filling the canoe, all of us trying to remain calm while yelling ideas on how to get off the rock. The guide kept assuring us that we would all be okay. It must have been a sight to see.

The guide on the single-hulled canoe noticed that we were stuck. He anchored his boat to a buoy and, telling the other riders to hold on, dove in the ocean and swam out to us. He climbed onto the rock and assessed the situation. He said that he'd have to bring another boat out to us to get us off the rock.

He once again dove into the ocean, swam back to his canoe, and guided that boat to shore, where everyone got out. He and another guy quickly paddled the canoe back out so those of us in the first hull could board and return to shore, lightening the load. But that meant getting out of the canoe we were in, navigating across the beached hulls, the rock, and the waves, and getting into the other canoe—all without falling in the ocean.

When it was my turn, I was apprehensive, but staying on the boat seemed riskier, so I stood up from my seat and climbed over the rim of the canoe. The rock was slippery, and the waves were still pounding. I held on to our guide's hand until he was stretched as far as possible, then grabbed hold of the second guide's hand until I reached the single-hulled canoe—which was bobbing up and down. I had to wait for it to drop down in the water before throwing my leg over the side and pulling myself in. I made it—phew!

When we reached the shore, we scampered out of the boat quickly. Paramedics were waiting to ask if we were all okay, which we were.

We were given towels, and after drying off we all hugged each other,so happy to have made it to shore. We were laughing and felt pride in surviving. I felt so alive!

We turned back to watch our original canoe, which the guide had managed to get off the rock, lighter with three of us out. The group was paddling back toward the shore, one side of the canoe sitting lower in the water.

There were cheers and more hugs and smiles all around once everyone had made it back safe and sound. We thanked the guides for their determination to get us back safely. That was an adventure we weren't expecting to have!

As we turned to walk away, I was struck by the funniest sight. Twenty or thirty of the hotel guests were sitting in lounge chairs on the beach, drinking their cocktails, just watching us without a care in the world—like it was an everyday thing to see a stranded canoe party rescued while they relaxed on their Hawaiian vacation.

Later that evening, we tossed around the question, "Is the safer boat really the safer boat?" What did a "safer boat" really mean? How was it quantified? At the beginning of the canoe trip, I went straight to what I was told was the safer option without question. But in the end, it wasn't really safer. In fact, if the single-hulled canoe had gotten stuck on the rock, it would have been much easier to dislodge.

It occurred to me that this concept is true in many areas of life. We often make choices to stay in a job or relationship because it's comfortable or because we are told that it's the right choice—the safer choice. Then we stick with the status quo, because at least we know what to expect from it. But this devil-you-know mentality comes from a place of fear: fear of change, fear of failure, fear of loss. You name it. So many people stay where they are and never make a change simply because they don't want to risk rocking the "safer" boat.

I wasn't immune to this—I'd stayed in my marriage and my IT job long past their expiration dates. I'd been holding on to a belief that society sold me, a belief that said I needed the marriage, the kids, the house, and the job in order to be successful. Sure, I was living comfortably, but I never found fulfillment in that life.

When I finally asked myself if that definition of success aligned with my definition of success, I found out that it didn't. Trying to force myself into that box was skewing my quality of life and dampening the gifts that I had to share with the world.

In my massage therapy work, I often talked to clients about their life: their jobs, relationships, hobbies, and so on. I saw many similarities between their current lives and how I'd lived in the past. Many of my clients worked in corporate careers. They hated their jobs, their coworkers, or their bosses.

I would often find myself asking them, "Why do you stay?"

The most common answer was "for the benefits." But what are "benefits" if you aren't actively benefiting from them? I understood why they were so focused on the someday that they were sacrificing their today; I had been there too. I knew what it was like to be stuck in the fear of *What if?* and scared into staying in the seemingly safer boat. But remember Garrett Gunderson's idea about a scarcity versus abundance mindset from Chapter 2? Living for today means taking a risk, but it also means opening yourself up to more abundance than you imagined possible.

There's a concept I learned about from my Strategic Coach program called the Gap and the Gain. The idea is that we are always trying to reach the horizon to find success. The problem is that the horizon is unattainable. It's always however far away you can see. It doesn't get closer to you as you move forward. If we think about our goals as the horizon, they feel unattainable, especially if we use "I'll be happy when ..." as a goal. This thinking can lead to feelings of despair and failure. This is called the Gap. I'm here looking out at the horizon, and it's never within my grasp.

However, if we measure from where we started, we can see how truly successful we are. For example, if I measure from my first cosmic alarm clock moment, when I woke up and decided to run the Seattle Marathon, I can see how far I've come. My life has been so much fuller and more challenging, exciting, and exhilarating since that day. This is the Gain.

The safer choice for me—the safer boat—would have been to stay at the job I hated and remain in my unfulfilling marriage. But that wouldn't have led me to the amazing experiences that I'm sharing with you in this book.

Recently I was teaching a class at my school, and the topic was self-care and body mechanics. We discussed ways to keep massage therapists injury-free for a long career. I told them about my adventure on the safer boat, and while we had a good laugh, the concept brought us to a point of introspection.

One student brought up the idea of emotional ergonomics. In the workplace, *ergonomics* describes an efficient workspace set up to decrease the chance for injury, especially repetitive injuries. Common examples are chairs that support sitting up straight or mice and keyboards that are sculpted for a more natural position of the hands. Emotional ergonomics is an interesting concept—designing one's environment and activities to promote well-being. This requires a person to take a critical look at their daily activities and environments and make adjustments that remove stress or negativity, promote positive emotions, and uplift their mindset.

A person cannot stay in a boat—even if it has been deemed the safer boat—if it causes stress and negativity and is making them sick and unhealthy. These are signals that it might be time to take a risk and move on, even if it feels uncertain and uncomfortable at first.

For me, that feeling of uncomfortableness is a nudge. It's my fear trying to dissuade me from progress, trying to convince me that it truly is safer in the boat I'm already in. Fear is the ultimate antimotivator. But I'm past letting fear stop me from moving forward. I can't let the waves move me; I have to be the one to Move the Boat, which is my fourth Pillar for Life.

I like to focus each day on living as fully and joyfully as possible during what time I have left on this planet. This is an idea that's been termed *mortality motivation*. I liken it to taking a car on the freeway and going as far and as fast as possible before I die. In life, we only have so much gas in our tank. We only have so much time. Living for the someday isn't an option—we have to live for now. This means sometimes leaving the safer boat and taking that risk so we can open ourselves up to opportunities—to really living life.

TWO

President John F. Kennedy said, "No American is ever made better off by pulling a fellow American down, and every American is made better off whenever any one of us is made better off. A rising tide lifts all boats."

When we approach life with the attitude of making the world a better place for everyone, we all win. I love the idea of collaboration rather than competition. I want to see everyone win. Being an athlete my whole life, I have reveled in the good stories of the underdog winning. I love cheering on my teammates, friends, and even other competitors. I want to create win-win situations, so I strive for a mindset of positivity, something that I learned to mirror from my mentors, who were relentlessly positive. Now my own clients, employees, and others tell me that my attitude is helpful and offers them hope for a better future.

During the COVID-19 pandemic, I was able to put this philosophy into action in a way that, even now, is creating new opportunities for school owners, massage therapists, and massage students.

The pandemic was difficult for many industries and affected the massage industry at a deep level. After all, massage has to be performed in person, and there's no way to maintain social distancing. Learning massage is also best done in person. So the new rules from the government shut down hands-on massage businesses overnight.

Like most business owners, I was immediately thinking of ways to pivot so my schools could remain open. I pulled from my IT background and created an online school, trained all staff and students on the new platform, and wrote a reopening plan that was shared by the American Massage Therapy Association, one of the largest massage organizations in the nation, to their membership list. I did this all within one week of being shut down.

I was as positive as possible with my staff and students. We did our best to set everyone up for success. We gave students kits to use at home for school projects, held special Zoom trainings, and brought in many guest speakers. I walked to the office most days to help me stay focused, and while there I would set a plan or teach classes. I encouraged students to find the good in their lives and be grateful. We made school-from-home as fun as possible.

I learned that in times of challenge we resort to our previous highest level of preparedness. My IT background and being a Quick Start helped me pivot and become a leader to other massage educators looking for help in a very uncertain time. But it was more than that too. Overcoming my personal struggles had made me more resilient. Losing my finger and the financial stress I'd been under during eighteen months of healing helped me weather the financial uncertainty in this new challenging time. The insights and tools I gained through my coaching programs not only helped me to grow as an individual but also allowed me to be a better leader to my students and peers while we navigated challenging times.

It was just like the high school basketball game with eight seconds left on the clock. You could say, *Only a measly eight seconds? What could possibly get done in so little time?* Or you could say, *In eight seconds, we can easily make the game-tying shot and take the game into triple overtime for the win.*

Staying positive was difficult to maintain in the long term, but there is no quit in me. The tension in the world was overwhelming with politics, the pandemic, and racial issues bubbling to the surface. My students felt it, and some of them dropped out of school due to the overwhelming stress. As we all waited for reopening guidance to keep ourselves, our clients, and our students safe, it became difficult for many massage businesses—especially if they were self-employed—to continue to pay office leases. Many independent contractors struggled to navigate state unemployment benefits.

Add to that the stress around mask and vaccine requirements and the worries of being out in public and catching or spreading the virus—it was a trying time. In Washington State, thousands of massage therapists left the field between 2020 and 2022. Many haven't returned.

Nationally, hundreds of massage schools closed, unable to sustain enrollment numbers, resulting in uncertain income. I spoke with one school owner in the Midwest who was losing money at their massage school in the two years prior to COVID-19. When the challenges they faced in the spring of 2020 exacerbated the situation, they were forced to close their school.

These closures created a massive shortage of licensed massage therapists around the US. At the same time, all the social distancing, isolation, and stress were making more and more people understand the benefit of and need for massage. The number of people who were experiencing touch deprivation exploded, and the demand for massage increased even more than the stressed system could handle.

Locally, we heard from different massage offices that were desperate to hire massage therapists. I would post a picture on social media of a graduating class and employers would make comments like, "Send them to us, we're hiring!" I thought, *Yeah, you and everyone else.*

How could I use my win-win attitude to help solve the problem? I thought there must be a way to benefit both my students and these desperate employers.

My team and I sat down and created the framework for a network of employers who exemplified qualities we believed were important for our students: proper classification of employee versus independent contractor, fair pay, good benefits, career progression, and supportive work environments.

The idea was that we could enhance my students' education by getting them hands-on practice through these employers. They would get to test out local businesses before they graduated, which would help them decide the next steps in their career. The employers would benefit because they would get some much-needed help as well as the ability to show off their offices to the students, who were prospective employees. In addition, the employers would support the massage school by participating in speaking events, attending community fairs, and offering externships. The expectation was that those in the network were as invested in our students' successes as we were.

Once we had a framework, we sampled the program with five massage offices close to both of my campuses. We had immediate buy-in from these local employers, and the program was a huge success. Since implementing the program, we've had employers who pay tuition for students, and they've sent students to us. Many of our students participate in the opportunities this program offers, including chiropractic, spa, clinic, and even pediatric oncology externships.

This has created a massive win-win-win situation for everyone: employers have the best opportunity to gain an employee fresh out of a top massage school, students have the best opportunity to find a job that will help them develop professionally before they even graduate, and Bodymechanics benefits by being the connector in the job market.

We were making huge strides at our school, but across the country, other massage schools were still having to close their doors. I wanted to help more than just my small corner of the market. I remembered how difficult it had been when I took over running my first massage school. I didn't know what was needed or what would work; everything was trial and error. But I had over a decade of experience and two thriving schools. I wanted to share what I'd learned and make it easier for other people looking to open a massage school.

So I created a massage school starter kit program that includes student curriculum, administrative support, instructor training, policies and procedures, and massage school management training. Those in this program wouldn't have to start from scratch like I did. They could create a thriving business right away and start helping people.

Offering training to new massage school owners in this collaborative way solves a big problem in the US: it helps provide careers to massage therapists and offers massage to the touch-starved and others in need. In addition, it propels massage therapists to a higher level of growth, especially if they don't have a retirement plan, they've been injured, or they are looking to solve a problem in their community.

During the pandemic was also when I created my Five Pillars for Life. When I look back at the actions I took during the pandemic, I hit all of my Five Pillars. I, like everyone else, was feeling shock and fear at the beginning. But I made a decision to *become un-numb*. I didn't want to just accept whatever was coming; I wanted to take decisive action to create better opportunities for myself.

During a time when the whole world seemed to be contracting in on itself, stagnating, and isolating, I felt an urgency to keep moving forward—*movement is life!* And I wanted to bring others with me. So creating movement with these new programs became "Hell yes!" movement for me.

I'm no stranger to loss, as you now know. But after losing two siblings and both my parents, I learned that the only way to keep going is to *follow your joy*. You have to do what lights you up, or you won't get out of bed in the morning. I wanted to remind people of how much we need one another and of how far we can get when we collaborate with a positive mentality.

Though it's always anxiety-inducing to try something new without any guarantee of how it will work out, I knew that these actions would help me grow. It was time to *move the boat* and to get others moving it with me too.

And finally, I'm a storyteller at heart, so I love to use story to connect to people. I knew that I could get people on board with these programs by sharing what I'd been through, and hopefully inspiring them to *tell their story* too, something I explore more in Pillar #5.

In the end, the Five Pillars for Life are about creating positive forward movement. Decisions come at us all the time, and it's useful to have a guiding structure that's based on where you want to be rather than restricted by your fears of what may happen. If an option you're considering doesn't fulfill every pillar, then it's an easy no. Plus, this way, you'll have more energy for the next thing that comes along and really lights you up.

THREE

Running has become an imperative for me. Running and training for my first marathon got me started on my healing path. Running also became a source of healing, first after the deaths in my family and later during the pandemic. It got me out of the house and reminded me that movement *is* life.

I ran my third marathon a week before my dad died in 2018, in St. George, Utah. I'm glad I was able to share this with him before he passed away, even though it was a very challenging run for me due to the amount of hills and lack of proper training.

In 2021 I ran my fourth marathon, the Boston Marathon, as a charity runner for the Massage Therapy Foundation. The marathon would have originally taken place in the fall of 2020, but, of course, the pandemic ended that dream, and my attention turned from marathon training to keeping my school, staff, and students moving forward through a very difficult time.

By spring of 2021 it was back on, and I had to get ready to run 26.2 miles by October. While in marathon training, I worked with a mindset coach, Kyle Brown. He helped me create a three-part mantra to say when I went out for a long run:

I am resilient.

I am a cheetah.

I always reach my goals.

I know that I'm resilient. I have seen proof of this every day of my life. I have strength to rise above the challenges, adapt, and even thrive in the face of adversity. Resiliency helped me through the losses of my family. Resiliency helped me overcome physical, mental, emotional, and financial pain after I lost my finger. I. Am. Resilient.

I'm far from a fast runner, but for distance running, endurance is the name of the game. Though cheetahs are known as the fastest land animal, they also possess a remarkable ability to run long distances when chasing prey. They are masters of endurance. This idea helped me reach the finish line of the Boston Marathon, and it also seemed like a good exclamation point on the challenges the previous eighteen months brought my school and me. I. Am. A. Cheetah.

It's difficult to see the forest for the trees, as the saying goes, and that couldn't be truer when it comes to seeing your own progress. Looking back, though, I could see the proof through my lifetime of how I reached and exceeded my goals. I became a successful business owner. I bought a building. I learned how to become strong and capable again after losing my finger. Thinking of all these powerful moments was all I needed for motivation to complete one more goal. I. Always. Reach. My. Goals.

Training was a challenge during the pandemic—not because I got sick, but because I was under pressure to keep everything else going. I needed to be strong for my staff and family and to keep the business afloat. My weekly talks with Kyle helped me process what I was living. It felt super heavy at times to consider all of the things I was responsible for, and I knew I needed support to find relief from the stress. Having so much on my mind all the time impacted my training and sleep, and I knew that if I was suffering, I couldn't take care of everything and everyone that needed my help. Kyle helped fuel my positivity muscle, which kept me moving forward for myself and all those who relied on me.

I realized that even pre-pandemic I'd become isolated. Before the pandemic, our main location in Tumwater had over one hundred people a day coming through the doors, and plenty of them would come into my office for various odds and ends. I finally had an office built upstairs so that I could focus and get work done. The foot traffic ended suddenly, and while it was nice at first, I didn't realize how much I missed and was inspired by all those in-the-moment conversations. Then the pandemic hit, my staff started working from home, and everything felt even more lonely.

I learned that I wasn't on my own and that it was okay to ask for help. I reached out to my friends, mentors, and family, even when it made me feel vulnerable. I got a dog, which forced me to get outside and go for long walks. I learned not to isolate myself. I realized I couldn't do it alone—but that I could create an army of people who were just as passionate as I was about my mission to get people out of pain.

Immersion into meditation and breathwork through the heavy times was grounding. I adopted the mindset of doing the best I could, and as long as I did my best, I would be okay with that. Going on long walks and listening to audiobooks was helpful too. Since stepping into entrepreneurship, I had stopped reading fiction. Yet I found my brain wanted a diversion of fictional worlds during those difficult days. I once walked ten miles while listening to a good book. It felt restorative and relaxing.

I really enjoyed using my mantra and saying it to myself before every long run. I would pound my chest and say, "I am resilient. I am a cheetah. I always reach my goals." Saying those words helped me keep going when I wanted to stop.

Another favorite activity was to text someone before going on a long practice run and let them know I was dedicating the run to them. Then, when I got home, I would have a response that would fill my tank.

One day, I woke up feeling that I needed to send a message to my friend Charlie Engle.

Charlie is an ultradistance runner who once ran across the Sahara. Incredibly, he ran two marathons a day for 111 days to raise awareness of the need for water in Africa. Fun fact: this was made into a movie called *Running the Sahara* that's narrated by Matt Damon.

Anyway, I woke up that morning and decided to text Charlie: "Hi, Charlie. I haven't heard from you in a long time, and I hope you are well! I sure miss you. I'm getting ready to go run thirteen miles this morning, and I often remember your advice when I'm running—slow and steady! I'm dedicating this run to you. Have a great day."

When I got home, I had this message back from Charlie: "Yes! Always the best running plan! So amazing to hear from you. You won't believe this, but I just landed in Seattle last night."

We ended up having breakfast two days later, and he also came to the massage school to share stories with my students of overcoming adversity. This experience filled my motivation tank for months.

When October arrived, I knew I was as ready as I was going to be. Our charity team comprised four team members: Oliver from California, Kelly from New York, Richard from Illinois, and me from Washington. We met the day before the marathon for the first time in person. The morning started out cold and overcast. Due to the pandemic, we had to wear face masks on the bus to the start line in Hopkinton, Massachusetts. We were dropped off about a half-mile from the start line and had to walk the rest of the way.

Our small team found the portable bathrooms and got ready for the run. Because of the pandemic, there wasn't an "official start" to the run; we just started when we were ready. The four of us started together for the first couple of blocks and then slowly found our own rhythms and paces. I ran the 26.2 miles alone yet in a crowd of people for the entire race.

During the marathon, I felt so alive. I took one triumphant stride after another, joy radiating from my being. It was difficult, but there was never a moment when I thought I wouldn't complete the course. As I crossed the finish line of the October 2021 Boston Marathon, I threw my arms in the air and raised my head to the sky with a newfound clarity—resilient to the end, going the distance just like the cheetah, and reaching my goals.

FOUR

Sometimes when I tell my story, I feel a bit like Forrest Gump—my story keeps going and twists in ways that are reminiscent of his. As Forrest tells us, "Mama always, said life is like a box of chocolates. You never know what you're gonna get."

My story can sound unbelievable: this happened, and then this happened, and then *this* happened! People often gasp or put their hand over their mouth, especially when I get to the part of my story where I lost my finger. It's still hard to say it out loud because the way it happened was gruesome and caused a lot of trauma for me.

I think back to myself at three years old, cracking my chin open and needing stitches, with my dad at my side telling me not to cry so I could get an ice cream cone at the end. I see my mom cooking or sewing while watching football games on her little TV. I see myself idolizing Steve, playing catch for hours on end with his words still in my head: "If you throw like a girl, I'll hit you!" I love that my brother followed his dream to become a journalist, because he was an amazing writer. I have outlived him by twenty years so far.

I see Judi as a teenager, listening to the Beatles' "Hey Jude" or Billy Squier's "The Stroke" and see how different we were from each other. She was the raspberry yogurt to my vanilla pudding. I think of Janice and our nightly sleepovers, which were really about me being afraid to sleep alone. I get to see Janice several times a year. When we are together, we fall into old patterns from childhood and talk about our family.

I think of the four of us kids growing up and see our innocence, unaware of the sadness and pain that would overtake us for so many years. I think about how we got good at funerals—how to answer all the questions at the funeral home, how to write a compelling obituary, who brings what food to the service.

How do you recover from such loss?

For me, it involved constant forward movement. I think of that Steve Jobs quote, of how you can't connect the dots as you're looking forward. But looking back, I can see that the dots began connecting for my more intentional and powerful life when I listened to that first cosmic alarm clock inspiring me to run a marathon. For a year, my mantra was the same: *Don't even think about it. Get up. Get dressed. Go run.* So I did. During those early-morning long runs, I would process the loss of my family, and I chose to keep living my life for them, to honor them and never forget them.

That alarm clock moment changed me. I realize now that I began looking forward instead of backward. I ran many miles on the streets between five and six in the morning, outrunning my fear of death and setting the foundation for my future self.

When I became a student at Bodymechanics in 2005, I discovered a new side of myself that craved learning about the body. I was pulled into learning how to help others feel better about their future.

It wasn't until years later when Ashleigh wrote me a letter telling me how much the deaths in the family affected her and how she lived in fear for years that I realized the breadth of trauma in our family. She told me that while I was in massage school, she was afraid I had been in an accident if I was ten minutes later than usual coming home. She said that she kept a funeral outfit in the closet, prepared for the next blow to our family. But she also went on to say that she saw me changing and transforming and never doubted my success for a second.

Reading her words affected me deeply, and I realized that my story is also my kids' stories. This gives even more power to my desire to change lives, because it started with my daughters. To know that I was a role model to help my kids live an exceptional life for their kids is all the proof I need to show I'm on the right path. I'm living a life to show them longevity is possible.

Endless positivity is the beginning. No more speaking words of pain to the cells in your body. I learned that my thoughts led to my beliefs, which led to my actions. I had to change my thoughts from *I'm going to die before I'm forty* to *I'm going to live to one hundred and fifty!*

I have to speak this into my cells to make it happen.

When I made the decision to get a divorce, it set a chain reaction to the next level of growth. It was an extremely painful process to go through, but in some regards it has been one of the most transformational experiences in my life.

Losing my finger led me to greater opportunities, but I didn't see that amid the hellish and painful storm. Being behind on every bill personally and professionally was stressful. Having two houses in foreclosure felt overwhelming and embarrassing. Losing my profession was devastating.

I could have lain on the couch and given up. It would have been so easy to just file for bankruptcy and get some other job building someone else's dream.

But I couldn't do it. I'd had a taste of living the life I was meant for, and I didn't want to let it go. I made the difficult phone calls to creditors and asked for leniency. I figured out how to cover payroll every damned time. I learned how to live with my new hand.

It has taken time for me to reflect, and now I see how powerfully the dots have connected. At each stage of my growth there has been a great upheaval that forced me to shift. Finding the internal strength to do the hard things shows me that I can do it again if needed. This is how I learned that the hard times were actually the impetus that caused the shift to happen in the first place. It's like pulling a rubber band back as taut as it will go, almost to the breaking point, and then releasing it. Look how far it goes! It was the same for me, the difficulties launching me forward into greater success. All the time I'm making more dots that I believe will connect in the future.

In 2015, I was on a bus in Buenos Aires with the Maverick1000 group. I was sitting next to my good friend, Steve, sharing how difficult my life had been since my finger trauma. He stopped me and said words that forever changed my perspective.

"Shari, you realize the injury had to happen on your hand, right?" he said. "If the injury had happened anywhere else on your body, you would still be massaging. And even though you loved massaging, you would not have grown as much as you have since then."

He was so right. The losses became the impetus for growth. I had a burning desire to live life to the fullest, and I wasn't going to let losses slow me down. All the losses I'd experienced—from my brother, my mom, and my sister to my marriage and my finger— have propelled me forward. I have not let loss stop my growth. It would only teach me new ways to be strong.

My dots had connected to form a beautiful web of growth for me. Losing my family gave me a greater appreciation for living life to the fullest. Losing my finger forced me to expand my business in new ways. Getting divorced made me confront my financial instability and find a better path forward. I learned how to push through the glass ceiling and grow beyond what I could have imagined possible.

What I realized is that I was resourceful and determined to escape from the trappings of a full-time job that was not fulfilling anymore. As I began to build my own business and take control of my career, I found that the qualities that had once made me feel trapped in my old job were now some of my greatest assets. I was able to think creatively, adapt quickly to new situations, and take risks that others might shy away from. I also discovered a deep well of resilience and determination within myself that allowed me to persevere through the ups and downs of entrepreneurship. Looking back, I can see that the experience of being stuck in a job that wasn't right for me was a valuable lesson in learning to trust my instincts and take action to create the life I truly wanted.

Steve helped me see my own resilience and strength—a capacity we all have, and one that heals and transforms us, making growth possible. While the recovery process was difficult and painful, it also gave me the space and time to reflect on my goals and think about what kind of legacy I wanted to leave the world.

As a result, my focus shifted from my private practice and school to building something much larger and more impactful: helping more people than I ever imagined was possible.

It's common to feel like you aren't enough—earning enough, strong enough, or doing enough. This kind of thinking only holds you back, especially if you're comparing yourself to someone else's measuring stick of what success looks like.

Get rid of the measuring stick. Look back over the last week, month, or year and discover how much you have done and are doing. Start telling yourself you are doing enough, and you are strong enough—*you are enough*.

I had to stop and connect the dots from where I am today to see how much I have accomplished. Each time it feels like I'm struggling, I remind myself that pushing through to the other side means that the challenging moment will become another dot connecting me to the future I'm meant to live.

The real secret? You're exactly where you are supposed to be. You have everything you need; all you have to do is reach out and take it.

PILLAR #5

— Tell Your Story —

When I was a new massage therapist, one of my favorite instructors, Kevin, moved away and referred many of his clients to me. It was such an honor to care for his clients in a way that reflected the best that he taught me while I was in school.

One such client was Mike McGrady. I saw Mike each Saturday around two in the afternoon for several years. Mike was a journalist, most notably for *Newsday*, a newspaper on New York's Long Island.

Over our Saturday sessions, he shared with me his love of writing books. He wrote several notable books, including *A Dove in Vietnam* that detailed his experience as a journalist covering the Vietnam War. Mike worked on another book called *Ordeal*, an autobiography of Linda Lovelace based on six months of interviews with her where she shared the story of her life as a porn star.

Another story he shared with me was about a book he pulled together as a literary spoof called *Naked Came the Stranger*, in which he convinced twenty-five other top journalists to write their imagined "dirtiest sex escapades" in one week. Then he put them all together in an anthology that went on to be a huge bestseller. These stories showcased how even poorly-written romance novels were being accepted. He was offered over $500,000 to write a sequel, which he turned town—clearly the publisher making the offer didn't get the point the book was making! His follow-up book, *Stranger Than Naked; or How to Write Dirty Books for Fun and Profit*, served as an instructional manual for those wanting to get into writing that genre.

I loved working on Mike. We had great conversations about books, and he always asked me about which book I was currently reading, what I liked or didn't like about it.

I shared once that I had wanted to write a book since my preteen years. From that point on, every session Mike would inevitably get around to asking me, "Have you started writing yet?"

Every week I'd respond, "No, not yet. But I will someday!"

Then came the week in 2012 when his response to my answer was different. He said, "I'll be so disappointed if you don't write your book."

The week after he said that, I went on a trip to the Netherlands. While I was gone, Mike suffered a stroke and was hospitalized. Ultimately, he passed away. I wonder if, in that last conversation, he had a premonition of his impending health challenge.

I've never let his words go. *Mike will be so disappointed if I don't write my book* became its own kind of mantra that's lain heavy on my mind and heart for years.

Mike knew about my family, the loss of my siblings and my mom. He had a way of pulling stories out of me—a journalist until the end. Our conversations were real and personal, and a true connection was formed over the years I worked with him. He inspired me to write my story, and here I am today, sharing it with you.

I think when I was first sharing my desire with him, my story wasn't complete enough; I wasn't healed enough to help others grow. I had to realize that the loss of my finger caused a cascade of lessons and learning opportunities for me to grow to the level where I am today.

I had to connect the dots. I had to find my story. But mostly, I had to find my purpose.

Before I lost my finger, my desire to help people was focused on the physical aspect of pain. It wasn't until I lost my finger and went through the healing process that I really wrapped my head around the idea of a whole-being approach to healing. This means helping to heal physical pain, sure, but also mental, emotional, and financial pain. I set a mission to use my hands and my experience to help one million people physically out of whatever pain they were experiencing. The deaths in my family, my divorce, my traumatic finger injury, and two houses in foreclosure all led me to this purpose.

I had to do everything I could to heal so that I could become the person I needed to be to help as many people as possible. Telling my story and sharing the lessons I've learned along the way are part of my bigger purpose—to help people out of pain. My purpose has since expanded to building a framework for others to join this mission, sharing their own stories and spreading the healing as far as it can go.

You've already heard my story. But we all go through adversity at some point in our lives. Most people tend to keep their challenges inside, walking through life and acting as if everything is perfect.

Until someone opens up about their challenges, there's an assumption that everything is going well. But you never know what other people are going through.

With this in mind, I wanted my book to be a space for others to share pieces of their own stories too. So here are ten short stories written by my friends, family, clients, and mentors—all people who have supported me, learned from me, and become my community. These people are from all walks of life who have each experienced a moment when they had to be resilient and pivot in ways they hadn't planned.

JANICE RUPP LUNG

Janice is my younger sister. She was beside me through the deaths in our family. She has her doctorate in education and a master's degree in public health. She is brilliant, caring, and has a heart of gold.

You go through life as planned, right? You have your solid foundation, family, and school. You get your first job and graduate—all the things you're supposed to do, right? Well, that's what I did. I went to college and graduate school, got my first real job, and was living on top of the world.

Then out of the blue something comes along so completely off your radar that it knocks you off your rocker. That's what happened to me, at least. My big-hearted, larger-than-life big brother suffered a stroke and passed away—way, way too young.

Pivot? More like "What's the worst possible thing I could do right now?" Quit my job and move? Okay. I'll take the first crappy job that comes along and then quit that one in three months only to make another mistake.

Eventually your life gets back on track, right? You find your way back to balance, return to your happy place, and develop lasting relationships. Well, that's what I did. I was looking ahead to a doctoral dissertation, working again in my field, making plans, and just starting to feel normal again.

Then you're hit with a one-two punch so powerful you can't even stand. Well, that happened. My *literal* world's best mom, keeper of family traditions, hostess of holidays, maker and baker of all things divine received a cancer diagnosis and died three days later. While still in a fog of grief, I learned that my mentor, friend, and first and favorite boss *ever* lost his battle with depression and took his life.

Pivot? There are probably other ways to describe trying to plan a wedding without my mom. Take my next career step without my mentor. Smile through the tears. Walk around the gaping hole in my heart.

When you're good at going through life with plans, you get back to the plan, right? You keep going. You move on. I did, anyway, even though I hadn't even recovered from the loss of my brother, my mom, or my mentor.

Well, the universe always shifts again. At least it did for me. When the phone rang long after I had drifted off to sleep, I knew. I just knew. My "march to the beat of a different drummer" sister was gone. Killed in a high-speed car accident that stripped another family of their loved one and left behind my sister's young children, our already-fragile father, Shari, and me.

Pivot? No way. Too numb for such a strong word.

So what do you do when you've survived so much—too much—

and God decides you can handle more? When the pain in your left breast won't go away? And the little pea-sized lump is cancer? And you think you're going to die because cancer equals death, right? Well, I'll tell you what I did. I pivoted. I set my sights on surviving cancer—the surgery, the chemo, the radiation, the medication, the joyful side effects that accompany each little step along the way to survival. I left my well-planned life, dreamed big with my too-good-to-be-true life partner, and took the plunge into a whole new world of health and well-being. We packed up and shipped out.

Since coming to Boise in 2009, I've forgotten how many times I've pivoted. Returning to college for yet another degree. Building a house aligned with our values. Buying a retreat in the mountains. Selling the retreat in the mountains. Taking a job an hour away—at an air force base. And more.

You pivot, right? You try planning, and God laughs. Well, she laughed at me, anyway. So I learned to pivot.

MIKE WHITLATCH

I've known Mike for many years. When I first met him, he was in the most beaten-down-by-life circumstances of anyone I had met. He was recommended by a mutual friend as someone who could help rebuild my school website. He was basically talking me out of hiring him when he came in for our first meeting. We've had many conversations about entrepreneurship and opportunities over the years of our friendship. I'm really proud of how far he has grown. Building one's possibility muscle is very hard, but Mike did it.

There wasn't one particular thing that I had to overcome. It was a series of events personally and professionally that were devastating. I found myself working in a job that I hated, divorced and with a young daughter whom I saw according to the parenting plan established when I got divorced. I first left a high-paying job that I loved to live in the town where my daughter lived. I bought a house to provide a home for her on weekends and summer vacations. Once I made this major life change, my ex-wife moved again, taking my daughter away from me—again. I felt helpless. The courts weren't helpful, and I was stuck in a town where I didn't know anyone and making less money at a job I couldn't stand. I had responsibilities though, and it felt like I was stuck. I had closed down and didn't believe that something good could ever happen to me again. However, over the years, I was able to meet special people that led me to believe that my future was bigger than my past.

I began seeing a light of possibilities when I met entrepreneurs who were doing amazing things. I learned how they overcame struggles. I opened up and allowed people to see the real me and in turn help me see that there were possibilities for a better life. These events caused a chain reaction of meeting certain people at the right time. Looking back, I realize that if I hadn't been open to the possibilities of something better, I'd still be locked in a place that I hated. I was able to attend an entrepreneur event, and my eyes and heart were opened. I began to believe that it was possible for me to be happy again. Eventually I met Eric Lochtefeld, who would have the greatest impact on my future.

I forged a new path on my own, selling everything I owned and moving from Washington State to Arizona to start my Harley-Davidson rental and touring company in Sedona. Despite the challenges of my past, I could still create a future that worked for me.

DEANNA SYLVESTER

I met Deanna at a massage conference in Hollywood, California. We were meeting a mutual friend in a bar who was running late, so Deanna and I began to talk about the projects we were working on at the time. One thing led to another, and Deanna ultimately began working with me on several different projects in Washington and New Mexico. I have valued her friendship over the years.

The best and worst day of my life happened on the same day. Why it was the worst day of my life was obvious to everyone; my son was born on that day, and he died two hours later.

You probably can't imagine what it feels like to have your heart and your mind shatter into a billion pieces unless you have experienced your own child die in your arms. Nothing makes sense after that.

For months afterward I was in shock; I couldn't even string two coherent thoughts together. I was confused every morning when I woke up—how could my heart still be beating while being shattered at the same time?

And then one day I remembered how it was that the worst day of my life had also been the best day. I remembered how calm and peaceful my tiny baby boy was in the midst of such chaos. He was lying on my chest, and despite being surrounded by noise and busyness and distraught family members, he was the lotus flower in a swamp. It was the most beautiful sight I had ever, and will ever, see. It changed everything.

As I learned to navigate my grief, my capacity to move forward with the heaviness began to expand. I learned and practiced Insight Meditation (a type of mindfulness) every day. I saw that I was not in control of anything that happens, and somehow that was a huge relief to me! I began to take opportunities that came my way, when previously I would have second-guessed my ability or my readiness. I kept waking up, I kept breathing, and I realized that I wasn't just this grieving woman (although I still was that too).

I could go where I wanted and do whatever I wanted, because nothing scared me anymore. I wasn't fearless in the sense of being reckless, like I didn't care; it was more like a fearlessness of knowing I had already experienced the worst that life could throw at me— and I'd survived. After many years of practice, I finally decided to teach others mindfulness meditation, so we can talk honestly about the truth of impermanence and the truth of suffering and how we have this capacity to hold it all.

So now, whenever I have something challenging come up, or I begin to worry, or I think about how difficult the world can be, I just remember the radiant face of my beautiful baby boy, who remained calm and peaceful even at the moment of his own death, and that changes everything.

MELINDA WITTSTOCK

Melinda and I met at a Maverick1000 group event, and we became immediate Maverick sisters. She was the first American woman reporter for the BBC, and during the Gulf War she was reporting live from Afghanistan. How cool is that? That's part of how amazing she is.

She introduced me to Richard Branson and made sure to let him know I was a nine-fingered massage therapist, which led to an amazing picture of Richard holding his pinky up next to my hand with the missing pinky. Melinda is a badass serial entrepreneur, and I value her and her friendship so much.

I can't even count how many things I have overcome on my thirty-year journey as a five-time serial entrepreneur! If there is one thing you learn as the type of entrepreneur who pioneers to disrupt whole industries, it is that the only thing you can take for granted is constant change and inevitable failures along the way. You learn, as I have, that obstacles and failures are gifts that make you stronger, smarter, and savvier. I have several stories at different points in my career that I'd like to share.

LESSON 1
THE GIFT OF DEFEAT

This one I learned early. I was editor-in-chief of my daily student newspaper at McGill University in Montreal, Canada, and the student council government never liked it when we reported on them. So they decided to take away all our funding. That's when my entrepreneurial spirit kicked in. I created an advertising department. I had no idea how to do that or what it meant in practice, and I soon discovered we'd need to find a way to get distribution beyond the campus to the city as a whole. So I figured that out and then realized we needed content that would make the paper relevant to readers other than college students. With this in mind, I created the first-ever English-language entertainment listings for the city, with reviews of restaurants, theaters, music venues, and more. We were profitable and growing within six months.

LESSON 2
NEVER ACT IN FEAR

Many years later I was busy creating the first-ever mobile crowd-sourcing news app called NewsiT. It was 2010, before Instagram, and NewsiT had supported photo, video, and text sharing. Social media platforms like Facebook and Twitter had the beginnings of what we now know as the "filter bubble" problem, where people fall deeper into their own worlds of information based on what they follow and it becomes hard to separate truth from fiction, dis/misinformation, and conspiracy. Given the fact we had 500,000 people creating content, I innovated algorithms that would assess contributions for both relevance and reliability, effectively solving the fake news problem a decade early. This was incredibly hard to do, and we nailed it. The NewsiT team had not only established unique algorithms to assure accuracy of user-generated contributions but also mobile user interface (prior to Facebook's move to mobile), and so much more.

But as a female founder, I couldn't raise the capital I needed to grow it. It was incredibly painful and frustrating. And here is where I went wrong: I decided I would morph the company and its technology into a social media analytics company, using our algorithms instead to understand and evaluate people's social media to qualify them as leads and microinfluencers for business clients. The company became known as Verifeed, and what I thought would be easier was actually much harder.

We would supply incredible insights to major companies, but before long, we came to realize they didn't know how to implement the insights we were sharing. We got pushed further and further into being an agency and a business I simply didn't like because it got out of alignment with my purpose. It was a business born of fear, and every day it felt like pushing a boulder up a mountain. I hated it, and yet I kept pushing and pushing, partly out of obligation to my investors and team and partly because I'm not a quitter. But for every step forward, it felt like two steps back. Which brings me to ...

LESSON 3

WHEN TO DIG IN AND WHEN TO TAKE A DIFFERENT PATH

One day I was sitting with the Verifeed board chairman by a babbling brook. We'd gone for a walk in the woods to talk about the company. Suddenly he said, "You're doing the wrong thing." I was stunned. My whole world felt like it was turned upside down.

He said it again. "You're a media person. You're a creator. You do companies that are consumer-facing. This company is not in your heart. Stop."

I didn't know how I could just stop, but here was the board

chairman, an investor, telling me it was okay; he was okay with losing his investment so long as I was able to press pause and regroup into something truly in alignment with my heart and soul. Verifeed continued to be used by his company, but I took a break. I then launched a podcast about female entrepreneurship called Wings of Inspired Business, experimented with a few things, and ultimately found my ideal business, Podopolo, the interactive AI-powered podcasting app that is now disrupting a whole industry.

MELANIE SPRING

Melanie is another amazing female entrepreneur who will change the world of anyone she meets—me included. She taught me how to speak on stage at a live event and helped me refine my story for speaking events. She is a brilliant rebel who helps others step into their power.

I was the director of marketing at a DC-based agency and was feeling pretty solid about my role at just twenty-eight years old. I had asked for a raise and promotion and received it just before the economic downturn of 2008 was in full swing.

That was until one day when my boss called me into his office and asked me a question that would change everything: "What would you do if I couldn't pay you anymore?"

My answer: "I'd work for myself."

His final words still ring in my ears: "Great, you have thirty days."

Almost fourteen years later, I recognize that pivotal day was one of the biggest points in my life where magic began. I started my branding agency that would run successfully for eight years and then transitioned to being a full-time international keynote speaker traveling the world with my message of doing the work you're here to do. I can honestly say that his words were the push I needed, since I had been standing on the edge of the entrepreneurial cliff but was too afraid to jump. I am grateful for that quick conversation, yet sometimes I still wish I had been bold enough to jump myself.

NICHOLAS MONTOYA

Nick was a student of mine at the Santa Fe, New Mexico, campus. He applied for a full tuition scholarship, and when I read his story, I knew I had to choose him. I knew a new career would improve his life and the lives of his family members. When he graduated from the program, he spoke about how important it was for him to show his two sons that it is possible to follow your dreams and be happy in a career that you are passionate about.

During the pandemic, I was stuck at home. I felt jammed in a rut, not sure what I should do. I remember thinking I could do more with my life. I was tired of doing nothing and going nowhere. I decided to look for my career and show my boys you can follow your dreams.

I always wanted to help people and went through so many changes in what I wanted to do—from teacher to lawyer to physical therapist. I knew my purpose was to help others. I landed on massage therapy and decided to apply for a full scholarship to a new massage school. It was the best decision I ever made. I feel like my life has new purpose and that I am helping people.

If I can give any advice to people that are unsure of what they want to do in life, my advice would be this: Follow your heart. Do something you love. Listen to your true self. I was always told by everyone I needed a job, but I didn't want another job where I was underpaid and underappreciated. Find something you love, and you'll never work a day in your life. I wake up each morning now knowing that, even if I have ninety-minute massages all day, it's not work because I'm making a difference in someone's life.

The words that stand true in my eyes are a quote from author Nora Roberts: "If you don't go after what you want, you'll never have it. If you don't ask, the answer is always no. If you don't step forward, you're always in the same place." That is my mantra, and I hope it helps others to reach for their dreams.

DAVID MUNTNER

I've known Dave for years through the Maverick1000 group. Dave is always interesting to talk with, and he always asks questions that make me think about why I'm doing something or who I want to help with a new program I'm developing. We've had some insightful conversations over the years. I have to say that David is truly inspiring for the actions he has taken to pursue a career as a singer and songwriter.

While I spent many years performing behind the drum kit of my rock band, I was always yearning to be the singer.

The only problem?

I was discouraged by practically everyone I knew when it came to pursuing this.

A guidance counselor in college told me not to be a singer. I was told I had a terrible voice by my bandmates, my father, and even a few singing instructors.

Even though I wasn't sure I could ever succeed as a vocalist, I continued to develop my craft. Year after year, I went through various singing instructors and practiced in the shadows.

It was only after sharing a private demo of me singing (the right place at the right time) after years of hidden practice that a secret team of patrons decided to invest in my personal singer/songwriter career.

This catapulted me to release my own music, and at this point I've written and recorded over forty songs, toured the country, and gained hundreds of thousands of listeners. It's only the beginning, but all the positives here reflect the importance of continuing on your path—the one you know is for you—and not taking no for an answer.

YANIK SILVER

Yanik is the chief instigator of the Maverick 1000 entrepreneur group. When I first met him, I found him easy to talk with and a bit mischievous. He's on a big mission to "light one thousand suns"—which is his way of inspiring visionary leaders to light more suns, each with a goal to change the world for the better. I'm proud to be a sun, lit by Yanik's passion to make the world a better place.

I was in trouble.

I needed to make payroll and pay several vendors, but we were short $70,000.

Not good!

Normally I'm a pretty laid-back guy, but I was really pissed. Mostly I was just angry at myself for letting this happen. I don't usually have a temper, but I heaved a cereal bowl at my wall. Damn it!

I mean, how the hell could I not fix this? I pretty much had the Midas touch with all my business ventures before. But now something I cared so deeply and passionately about was going south ... and dragging my other businesses down along with it.

By way of background, I'd had eight different products and services that hit the cumulative seven-figure mark in the online space—so I knew a thing or two about what works—but the playbook had changed for me. How did I get here?

From the outside, most people would think I had achieved total success. I was making a *lot* of money online by truly helping people. I had built up a great reputation in the marketplace, drove a cool car, had an incredible family, lived in a nice neighborhood, and so on. Don't get me wrong, I was (and still am) extremely grateful and appreciative for everything I had, but I just wasn't totally happy.

Maybe you've experienced the same thing: You've "made it" but realize there's something more. Perhaps you have a nagging notion you can't shake that you were designed for greater things. You want to fully put *all* your talents, passion, and resources into something bigger. Maybe you discount all of this as burnout, but it's much bigger than that. It usually starts with a sense of discontent or frustration. Or a sense of being bored with what's going on in your business.

Of course, you could continue to plug away, but you know in your heart that will just slowly eat away at your soul. You need to make a leap into the next chapter but aren't sure you can without sacrificing everything you've built. And that lack of enthusiasm carries over to your team, your work, and your customers. Truly everything. You're either going to subconsciously sabotage your business or your life to make it change unless you're aware of what's going on. That's when you go looking for creative (and sometimes self-destructive) outlets to compensate for not being totally engaged. Following your true heart's calling is never wrong—but it is frequently scary!

I know because I've been there. That's why, a little over eight years ago, I made my next biggest transition from "just" being an internet marketer teaching and selling my own products. My criterion was pretty simple. I asked myself the big question: "Will I be happy and totally fulfilled ten years from now doing what I am doing now?" The answer was a resounding and booming "NO!"

I knew my greatest contribution lay somewhere else with everything so far being the setup for something greater. I had stopped growing and stopped being passionate about what I was doing. These frustrations led me to do a lot of journaling and reflection.

Originally, my idea that came from journaling stemmed from my own desire to hang out with other successful entrepreneurs and do wild adventures together. I'd combine it with business building and something charitable mixed in. I wanted to combine everything I really liked together and called the company Maverick Business Adventures, with the appropriate acronym of MBA. I had bootstrapped my first venture with a couple hundred bucks out of a one-bedroom apartment, but for this one, I was going to do it right.

I would hire a real team, we would go first-class on the branding, and I'd really invest in the business in all the ways I never did before. I'm a big believer in forced deadlines to create action, so I set our first Maverick Business Adventures trip to go Baja racing in Mexico in January 2008. Baja racing is one of my favorite adventures and holds deep personal meaning for me. My friend, Corey Rudl, first introduced me to this experience only a few months before a tragic racing accident claimed his life.

This kind of wild adventure developed powerful connections in a totally different setting. We ended up becoming friends with several high-level CEOs (including one NASDAQ-listed company) who were also on the trip. Corey and I talked about business and life and a lot about wild adventures we wanted to go on, like flying MiGs together. Unknowingly, that trip was a big spark to create Maverick Business Adventures.

We lost about $30,000 on this first trip, and then in short order, I sunk about $400,000 in before Missy, my wife, finally asked what I was doing. I was so excited about this project that I made some expensive hiring mistakes, bringing in six-figure people before we needed them or ones who couldn't perform within the resources of a startup. What's more, I didn't stop soon enough to evaluate the business model. It was all about the trip, and the margins on an excursion are so much thinner than selling information as I had before.

There was a small membership fee but not really enough to cover everything we were doing and the team I had hired. I rationalized by telling myself it was an investment because this was a different type of business and that it might take some time to break even. I've learned the universe will continue to bonk you on the head with increased severity if you don't figure it out. I had done a lot of financial juggling, like having one company pay for a sponsorship for another instead of letting it stand on its own two feet.

But the day I chucked my cereal bowl at the wall across the room, I knew I had to face reality. It took selling my Aston Martin sports car to pay for payroll to get my attention. (And I still have a small dent on the kitchen wall as a reminder to me.) It was pretty much either selling my car or my ticket to space on Virgin Galactic for extra cash to help the company through the crunch. I figured cars come and go—but a ticket to space is pretty awesome. After finally realizing the downward financial trajectory of the company, it forced me to change up the business model significantly. We adjusted the cost structure while also updating benefits and services to members to include several structured retreats per year. It was a longer process than I thought, but we did turn the company around, and now I'm proud to say it's solidly in the black.

Looking back at this experience, I'm incredibly grateful for not getting it right the first go around. Is your *why* big enough? I'm thankful for those experiences because it forced me to truly decide if the vision for what we were building was worth it or not. If I was just creating a fun adventure company, then, no, it wasn't worth it. It was my love for a bigger mission that kept me going to figure out how to make it work. I realized what I originally wanted to build wasn't nearly as impactful or compelling as the revised vision for the Maverick.

ERIC LOCHTEFELD

Eric is one of the most inspirational people I know. I've known him for several years now, and he has a heart of gold. He has three primary passions: to inspire friends to discover and pursue their bliss dreams; to host incredible events in beautiful, luxurious places; and to write inspirational stories. Attending one of his incredible events at Bliss Island on the Big Island in Hawaii was a game changer for me—and it's one of the reasons I wrote this book.

At the start of 2022, I knew I was stuck, but I did not know why. After twenty-five years living the life of a successful entrepreneur, I felt restless, like a caged lion. I had slayed every major dream I set my sights on. My companies had generated hundreds of millions of dollars. I had everything I ever wanted and needed. I was even coming off an amazing four-year journey where I pursued joy as my highest value, producing a level of aliveness I did not know I had in me—yet, I was sad. What gives?

This went on for nearly three months when my good friend, colleague, and world-class therapist Dr. Heather Dee Frankovich flew into town to help me run a personal development retreat. As the cohost, I did not expect to participate like our customers, but she asked everyone (me included) to bring a photo of when they were a child to the retreat. I didn't have any on me, so I called my mother and asked her to pick one out. I received a cute photo of me as a three-year-old sporting a red onesie at a beach on vacation with my parents in California.

When the workshop using the photo began, Heather asked us all what we could teach our child self. All of the sudden, I was *that* child again, at the very moment before that picture was taken— right before the trauma I didn't even remember until just then! Minutes after that photo was taken by my mom, my dad came out to the beach to have a serious conversation with her. Even as a three-year-old, I somehow heard all of their adult conversation, and the trauma from that day made it into my nervous system.

What was the traumatizing conversation? Well, to you as an adult reader, it may not seem too big of a deal. But I was a three-year-old in his cognitive years unable to differentiate between trauma with a capital *T* and trauma with a lowercase *t*. My dad's boss had promised him time off and had unscrupulously called him back to work on day two of our family vacation. My dad was telling my mom he had to leave to fly back to work.

Not that big of a deal, right? Well, for a three-year-old who loves his papa and cherishes hunting for shells every morning with him and hanging out all day at the beach, this might as well have been a death sentence. Recalling this in the workshop is when my breakthrough occurred. I realized that my three-year-old self made a life-changing decision that day. I decided to become an entrepreneur, become wildly successful, and take my parents on epic vacations as much as I wanted.

My realization as a fifty-year-old man who had fulfilled that dream was that I didn't want to be an entrepreneur anymore. I wanted to be an artist—a playwright, in fact. The reason for my pain was that I felt I would be betraying the commitment my three-year-old self made to always be my own boss and never let anyone do to me what my dad's boss had done to him that day. I needed permission to become something else from my three-year-old self.

The universe is astounding!

DARYL MURROW

Daryl is a good friend whom I met at a local networking event. Students at my school benefit from his gift, which is to help business owners create and use systems that help them grow. His "Unstoppable badass community" inspires and lifts local entrepreneurs up.

From early childhood, I developed the belief that I was unworthy, undeserving, and never good enough, and I struggled with this for nearly fifty years. I believed love, success, and happiness belonged to "lucky" people.

To compensate for this unworthiness, I turned into a people-pleaser—always putting the needs and desires of others first. Because of my lack of worthiness, I had difficulty standing up for myself that led to situations where I allowed people to take advantage of me.

I owned a small record store and had a couple of employees working for me.

As a business owner, I would shy away from meeting other business owners and joining networking groups because I was afraid people would discover how unworthy I really was, and I was constantly fearful I would be exposed. I lived in a mental prison of anxiety and despair that often manifested into anger and depression.

It wasn't until I attended a self-help seminar that I became aware of these self-limiting beliefs and was able to challenge them for the first time. Although this may sound a bit ridiculous, when I realized I did have worth and value, I felt absolute joy and a level of freedom I had never experienced before. It was quite profound for me.

Now, dear reader, it's your turn to tell your story.

EPILOGUE

Finding resilience in the midst of a storm is hard work. I hope that my story and the stories of my friends inspire you to realize you can move past the challenges you are faced with.

After journeying through my Five Pillars for Life—Become Un-Numb, Movement Is Life, Follow Your Joy, Move the Boat, and Tell Your Story—and hearing the powerful testimonies of resilience from friends who have faced and overcome their own challenges, we arrive now at a threshold.

This threshold is not an ending but rather a beginning—a place where the last page of this book becomes the first page of your next chapter. I invite you to pause and consider the essence of what this journey has been about.

What have you learned about the nature of strength that lies within you in overcoming challenges you may be facing? Have these insights shifted your perspective on the daily dance of your life?

What I hope for you, dear reader, is that the stories and principles laid out in these pages have sparked a flame—a flame that will light your path as you forge ahead, carrying the light of purpose. My vision has been to help one million people out of pain, and I hope that in telling my story, you are inspired to make a change to finally shed the negative emotions and grow.

As you move forward, perhaps armed with new knowledge and a renewed sense of self, consider what you will take with you. Which pillar resonates with you the most so that you can find your resilient strength?

And finally, my deepest wish for humanity—a wish that has been refined and clarified through my own challenges and triumphs—is simple yet profound: may we all find the courage to live authentically, to embrace the full spectrum of our experiences, and to extend compassion to ourselves and others as we navigate the complexities of the human condition.

As we say goodbye to the stories enclosed in these pages, I leave you with these reflections: You have everything within you to change your future. This is not just a call to action; it is an affirmation of your inherent potential and power. The stories you've read are mirrors reflecting the resilience that also resides within you. Remember that each day offers you an opportunity to apply joy, movement, and your authentic story into your existence to help others improve their lives.

What's next for you is a story yet to be written. How will you use the insights from this book to change your story? How will your unique journey help others improve their lives? Your next steps are yours to choose, and in them lies the possibility to not just dream of a different future but to create it.

With each breath and each step, you have the power to move the boat of your life in the direction of your dreams. Remember, the most profound journeys often begin with a single, purposeful step. Take that step, un-numb yourself, and live fully in the movement that is life itself.

ACKNOWLEDGMENTS

Writing this book has been a journey of growth and discovery, and I'm deeply grateful for the incredible support I've received along the way.

First and foremost, I want to thank my family. To my daughters, Hayley and Ashleigh, your love and laughter remind me daily of what truly matters. To my sister Janice, you are my hero and best friend and your unwavering belief in me provided the foundation upon which this book was built. To my parents, Sharon and Jack, and my siblings Steve and Judi, I miss you every day. I'm grateful for the lessons I learned from you and your life. I love you.

A heartfelt thanks to the team at World Changers Media, Bryna Haynes and Maggie Mills, whose keen eye and insightful feedback have refined my work beyond measure. I have endless gratitude for World Changers Media for believing in this book and helping it find its way into the world.

As a new massage therapist in 2006, I enjoyed weekly conversations with a special patient, Mike McGrady, who was a published author himself of several *Washington Post* top 10 books. We would talk about books and writing, and I told him that I had wanted to write a book since childhood. Each week, he would ask me if I had started writing, and I would say not yet. The last session with him, he told me that he would be so disappointed if I didn't write a book. He passed away shortly after telling me that. So, to Mike, one of my first encouragers, I did it!

Special thanks to my dear friends for sharing their adversity stories for my book: Janice Rupp Lung, Mike Whitlatch, Deanna Sylvester, Melinda Wittstock, Melanie Spring, Nicholas Montoya, David Muntner, Yanik Silver, Eric Lochtefeld, and Daryl Murrow. Your stories are inspiring and will help countless people overcome adversity in their lives.

To the Mavericks, your encouragement and shared passion for growth has been a constant source of motivation. I mention many stories in this book of my time with the Mavericks, and I can say with certainty that the growth I experienced through this incredible entrepreneur group changed my life for the better.

To my Bliss Island family, deep gratitude to Patrick Combs and Eric Lochtefeld for creating the spark for me to birth this book. I've had many Cosmic Alarm Clock moments, but the day I woke up with a message from the universe that led to writing this book will forever give me goosebumps.

Finally, to my readers, thank you for taking this journey with me. I hope this book inspires you as much as the process of writing it has inspired me.

ABOUT THE
AUTHOR

Shari Aldrich is a seasoned massage therapist, a visionary entrepreneur, and a mentor to massage professionals nation-wide. As the founder of a successful massage school, Shari has transformed personal adversity into professional triumph. The loss of a finger not only reshaped her approach to massage therapy but also taught her the invaluable skill of elevating her business acumen to work on her business rather than in it.

Her journey is marked by resilience in the face of profound loss, having experienced the untimely deaths of two siblings, the sudden passing of her mother, and the loss of her father. These personal trials have imbued her with a deep empathy and understanding, which she brings into every aspect of her work and teachings.

Beyond her professional life, Shari is a devoted mother to two daughters, who proudly stand by her side in the family business. Her role as a grandmother to seven grandchildren adds yet another layer of joy and fulfillment to her life, infusing her with a passion for nurturing growth, whether with family or her community of aspiring therapists.

Shari's commitment to healing, education, and family shines through in her efforts to empower the next generation of massage therapists. She is dedicated to creating spaces where healing is not only a profession but a way of life, passing on her legacy of resilience and care.

In her writing and teaching, Shari draws on her experiences to guide others on a path to professional independence and personal healing. Her approach is holistic, heartfelt, and grounded in the belief that every individual has the capacity to overcome, evolve, and enrich the world with their unique gifts.

ABOUT THE PUBLISHER

Founded in 2021 by Bryna Haynes, WorldChangers Media is a boutique publishing company focused on "Ideas for Impact." We know that great books change lives, topple outdated paradigms, and build movements. Our commitment is to deliver superior-quality transformational nonfiction by, and for, the next generation of thought leaders.

Ready to write and publish your thought leadership book with us? Learn more at www.WorldChangers.Media

Made in United States
North Haven, CT
28 June 2024

54182353R00095